ENGLISH ESSAYS

BLACKIE & SON LIMITED
66 Chandos Place, LONDON
17 Stanhope Street, GLASGOW

BLACKIE & SON (INDIA) LIMITED
103/5 Fort Street, BOMBAY

BLACKIE & SON (CANADA) LIMITED
TORONTO

ENGLISH ESSAYS

A REPRESENTATIVE ANTHOLOGY

EDITED BY

W. CUTHBERT ROBB, M.A.(Hons.)

Principal Teacher of English, Hawick High School

BLACKIE & SON LIMITED
LONDON AND GLASGOW

First published 1940
Reprinted 1942, 1943 (twice), 1945,
1946, 1948

Printed *in Great Britain by Blackie & Son, Ltd., Glasgow*

PREFACE

The thirty-four essays in this book are a representative selection from the vast amount of material available from the sixteenth century to the present day. Almost every type and style of essay is included, and selection has been dictated by my own experience of what is likely to be most useful in the Secondary School and most appreciated by the pupils.

The introductory historical and critical note contains material that I myself have found of the greatest value in school, and I hope that others (both teachers and pupils) will also find it so.

The Biographical Notes which are included in the text are for the most part simply facts conveniently summed up. The short Critical Notes at the end of the book may afford some guidance to pupils tackling the exercises which are printed along with them.

W. C. R.

Hawick,

ACKNOWLEDGMENTS

The Editor and Publishers make grateful acknowledgment to the following for permission to reprint copyright material from the works named:

Mr. Lloyd Osbourne and *Charles Scribner's Sons* for " Walking Tours ", " A Plea for Gas Lamps ", and " Child's Play " from *Virginibus Puerisque* by Robert Louis Stevenson.

Mr. C. D. Medley for " Old Booksellers " by Augustine Birrell.

The Executors of the late E. V. Lucas and *Methuen & Co., Ltd.* for " Her Royal 'Tumnal Tintiness " from *Old Lamps for New* by E. V. Lucas.

Mr. Hilaire Belloc and *Methuen & Co., Ltd.* for " On Cheeses " from *First and Last* by Hilaire Belloc.

Miss Collins and *Methuen and Co., Ltd.* for " On Running after One's Hat " from *All Things Considered* by G. K. Chesterton.

Mr. Robert Lynd and *Methuen & Co., Ltd.* for " The Unexpected " from *The Gold Fish* by Robert Lynd.

Mr. E. V. Knox and *Methuen & Co., Ltd.* for " Witches and Whatnot " from *This Other Eden* by E. V. Knox.

Mr. Christopher Morley and *Jonathan Cape Ltd.* for " On Doors " from *Safety Pins* by Christopher Morley.

CONTENTS

INTRODUCTORY NOTE — THE ESSAY

What is an essay?

There have been many attempts to define the essay, and no one of them has been entirely satisfactory. To say that it is merely a short piece of prose is certainly not sufficient, for prose may be of many different kinds; and even so far as it goes it is inaccurate, for such an essay as Locke's *Essay concerning the Human Understanding* is anything but short. Nor can one fairly restrict it to any particular type of prose, for, as even this small anthology shows, essays may be of widely different types — philosophical, descriptive, narrative, argumentative, and so on. One comes fairly near a definition when one postulates that the essay must express the writer's personal opinions of something; but that in itself is hardly a definition. It has been said that a dog is any animal which another dog instinctively recognizes as a dog: perhaps it would be wisest to say that an essay is any piece of writing which a reader of essays instinctively recognizes as an essay, and let it go at that.

The essay is no newcomer in the literary world. It is usually taken as dating from Montaigne; but it is worth while glancing back a little farther — as far back, indeed, as the Classics. The Dialogues of Lucian are nothing else but essays in dialogue form; and, going even farther back, the treatise of Aristotle on Tragedy is

an essay, and one of the greatest ever written. Nor did
the Romans lack essayists, though some of them, like
Horace and Lucretius, wrote their essays in verse. But
for practical purposes, we may bow to convention by
beginning our survey with Montaigne.

Montaigne was a French philosopher who lived in the
middle of the sixteenth century, and, mainly to clarify
his own opinions, wrote what he called Essais (i.e. attempts) to express his thoughts on many subjects. His
works were translated into English by John Florio in
1603, under the title of *The Essays, or, Morall, Politike,
and Millitaire Discourses of Lo: M. de Montaigne.* These
gained an immediate popularity in England; indeed,
along with Plutarch's *Lives* and the Bible, of which the
Authorized Version was published in 1611, they enjoyed
perhaps wider popularity than any other book in England in the early seventeenth century, and exercised an
influence which must be unequalled over subsequent
English literature. They appealed to the English philosopher Bacon, who had already published several works
of philosophy (and, some would have us believe, a number
of plays under the sobriquet of William Shakespeare);
and Bacon turned to essays. His first essays appeared in
1597 (he was a French scholar, and had already read
Montaigne in French before that), to be followed by
other and larger editions in 1612 and 1625.

It must not, however, be thought that Bacon was a
mere imitator of Montaigne. Both men, it is true, wrote
essays: but there the resemblance almost stops. Montaigne, in his essays, is discursive almost to the point of

long-windedness: Bacon gives us the outstanding example of brevity in literary style. Montaigne wrote in a way that could be understood by everybody: Bacon wrote for the educated classes alone — men who could " chew and digest " what they read. A glance at the essays in this anthology will show the vast difference between the essays of Bacon and those of any of his successors; indeed, to the writers of to-day, a Baconian essay is not so much an essay as a summary capable of being expanded into a much longer essay. That this began to appear very soon is apparent from the fact that his next great follower, Cowley, developed a much more discursive style. Cowley was not one of the really great essayists, but he deserves inclusion in any anthology because he was the link between Bacon and the essayists of the eighteenth century. He is not so discursive as Addison and Steele, but he is more discursive than Bacon: he is not so outspoken and incisive as Swift, but he is more so than Bacon. He forms, as it were, a bridge between the seventeenth- and eighteenth-century essayists. Swift carried the change a step further: and the stage was set for the appearance of the great essayists Addison and Steele.

The development of the essay in the hands of these two masters of English was the result of the development of newspapers, or rather magazines. Since the Restoration, life had been much pleasanter and gayer than hitherto: men craved amusement, and they found it at first in plays, coffee-houses, and fine clothes. But they required more than that. Culture had spread through the country, and now almost all men could read: the time was ripe for the appearance of magazines with topical essays, and the essays came. The *Tatler* appeared in 1709, the *Spectator* in 1711; and in their train came a host of other periodicals, including the *Gentleman's Magazine* in 1731, the *London Magazine* in 1732, and Johnson's *Rambler* in 1750. Most of them were short-lived, but they served their purpose. To meet their needs, the periodical essay was devised — a short article of wide interest and appeal: it caught the public fancy, and became a model for all subsequent essayists. The immortal Spectator Club was founded by Addison and Steele; and essays on the imaginary members, men of widely different interests, appeared regularly every few days. The essay had radically changed its form, and though it has since developed in many different directions, the essay of Addison and Steele, and not that of Bacon, is the real ancestor of the essay of to-day.

Of the later development of the essay, little need be said here. Changing times have brought changing needs with them, and the essay has changed with the times; but the great essayist of to-day is not so very different from the great essayist of a hundred years ago, or, for that matter, of two hundred years ago. Perhaps the most obvious difference is in the average length of the essay. Those of Addison and Steele were quite brief (not so brief indeed as those of Bacon, but much less compact): with the spread of education and increased facilities for reading, longer essays became for a time more popular: then the rush and hurry of modern life shortened the essay again, as it did the other forms of literature, and the essay of to-day is more frequently under three thousand words than over it. It is perhaps also true to say that the essays of to-day treat more widely different subjects than the essays of any previous age: that too is natural, for knowledge and interests have spread and widened as never before; and though it happens that this anthology contains no essay by a woman, the emancipation of women has left its mark by bringing a myriad not only of readers but also of writers into being that were never dreamed of in the days of Bacon.

So far I have written only as a reader of essays to readers of essays: but I think this foreword would not be complete without a word to those who will try, however humbly, to follow in the steps of the great writers whose works furnish the body of this book. Imitation, they say, is the sincerest form of flattery; and it is true, if trite, to say that the young readers of to-day are the essayists of to-morrow. We all have our own thoughts, even the humblest of us. We express them in speech a hundred times a day: and it should not be such a very difficult task to express them in writing instead. When we do so, we write an essay: but — and this is a very big but — when we search out, arrange, and express even the greatest thoughts of others, we do not write an essay, unless we leaven the composition with our personal opinions. That is the commonest fault of the earnest young writer. It is shyness perhaps which makes him feel that his own thoughts are not worthy of expression, and he slavishly copies down the sentiments of one

greater than himself, changes the order, alters a word
here and there, hands it to his mentor, and hopes for the
best. That is misplaced humility: did he but know, his
own thoughts are a hundred times more valuable, simply
because they are his own. Minds differ as do finger-
prints, and every mind has its own impressions: even
the humblest expression of personal opinion is many
times more valuable than a slavish repetition of what has
already been said, probably much better, by someone
else.

That too is why it is worth while to approach the subject from a new angle if at all possible. It is true that
most things have been said before; but it is always
possible to say an old thing in a new way. The reader
will find, for example, that at least three of the essays in
this book deal with journeys; but in these essays are
expressed the thoughts of three different minds on the
same subject — and how they differ, even when the
sentiments of the writers are in complete agreement!
That is because the personality of the writers makes
itself felt in whatever they write; and while, in our
earliest attempts at expressing ourselves, we are perhaps
occupied with the intricacies of grammar and syntax so
much that we have little thought to spare for the choice
of words, once that initial stage is over a personal style
appears without forcing and as it were of its own accord.
There is no royal road to writing: one can only learn
to write by reading much and carefully, writing much
and even more carefully, re-reading one's efforts with a
very critical eye, and writing once more. In this antho-

logy there are examples of almost every type and style of essay: if the careful reading of them can inspire even a few to produce essays of their own comparable even to the least perfect essay in this book, the editor will feel that the labour of compilation has not been in vain.

FRANCIS BACON, LORD VERULAM

(1561–1626)

Francis Bacon, who was born in London, was well educated
and took up law as a career. In 1583 he entered Parliament as
member for Melcombe Regis, and though he did not enjoy the
favour of Queen Elizabeth, under James I he advanced rapidly,
becoming Solicitor-General in 1607 and Attorney-General in
1613. In 1621 he was impeached and condemned for accepting
bribes, and this ruined his political career.

Meanwhile he had written much in both Latin and English
— mainly works of philosophy, but also his Essays. It is by
these that he is remembered, though their volume is small.
Ten of them appeared in 1597; another edition with 38 was
issued in 1612, and the final collection of 58 in all in 1625.
Though no doubt he was influenced by Montaigne, his essays
differ from those of Montaigne in their extreme conciseness,
resembling them only in that they give us his personal opinions
on the subjects which they treat. His Latin works are mainly
heavy philosophical treatises; but they, in conjunction with
his essays, have gained him the reputation of being the founder
of modern methods of thought.

OF TRUTH

What is *Truth*; said jesting *Pilate*; And would not
stay for an Answer. Certainly there be, that delight in
Giddinesse; And count it a Bondage, to fix a Beleefe;
Affecting Freewill in Thinking, as well as in Acting.
And though the Sects of Philosophers of that Kinde be
gone, yet there remaine certaine discoursing Wits, which
are of the same veines, though there be not so much

Bloud in them, as was in those of the Ancients. But it
is not onely the Difficultie, and Labour, which men take
in finding out of *Truth*; Nor againe, that when it is
found, it imposeth vpon mens Thoughts; that doth
bring Lies in fauour: But a naturall, though corrupt
Loue, of the *Lie* it selfe. One of the later Schoole of the
Grecians, examineth the matter, and is at a stand, to
thinke what should be in it, that men should loue *Lies*;
Where neither they make for Pleasure, as with Poets;
Nor for Aduantage, as with the Merchant; but for the
Lies sake. But I cannot tell: This same *Truth*, is a Naked,
and Open day light, that doth not shew, the Masques,
and Mummeries, and Triumphs of the world, halfe so
Stately, and daintily, as Candlelights. *Truth* may perhaps come to the price of a Pearle, that sheweth best by
day: But it will not rise, to the price of a Diamond, or
Carbuncle, that sheweth best in varied lights. A mixture of a *Lie* doth euer adde Pleasure. Doth any man
doubt, that if there were taken out of Mens Mindes,
Vaine Opinions, Flattering Hopes, False valuations,
Imaginations as one would, and the like; but it would
leaue the Mindes, of a Number of Men, poore shrunken
Things; full of Melancholy, and Indisposition, and
vnpleasing to themselves? One of the Fathers, in great
Seuerity, called Poesie, *Vinum Daemonum*; because it
filleth the imagination, and yet it is, but with the shadow
of a *Lie*. But it is not the *Lie*, that passeth through the
Minde, but the *Lie* that sinketh in, and setleth in it, that
doth the hurt, such as we spake of before. But howsoeuer
these things are thus, in mens depraued Iudgements,
and Affections, yet *Truth*, which onely doth iudge it
selfe, teacheth, that the Inquirie of *Truth*, which is the
Loue-making, or Wooing of it; The knowledge of

Truth, which is the Presence of it; and the Beleefe of *Truth*, which is the Enioying of it; is the Soueraigne Good of humane Nature. The first Creature of God, in the workes of the Dayes, was the Light of the Sense; The last, was the Light of Reason; And his Sabbath Worke, euer since, is the Illumination of his Spirit. First he breathed Light, vpon the Face, of the Matter or Chaos; Then he breathed Light, into the Face of Man; and still he breatheth and inspireth Light, into the Face of his Chosen. The Poet, that beautified the Sect, that was otherwise inferiour to the rest, saith yet excellently well: *It is a pleasure to stand upon the shore, and to see ships tost upon the Sea: A pleasure to stand in the window of a Castle, and to see a Battaile, and the Aduentures thereof, below: But no pleasure is comparable, to the standing, vpon the vantage ground of Truth:* (A hill not to be commanded, and where the Ayre is alwaies cleare and serene;) *And to see the Errours, and Wandrings, and Mists, and Tempests, in the vale below:* So alwaies, that this prospect, be with Pitty, and not with Swelling, or Pride. Certainly, it is Heauen vpon Earth, to haue a Mans Mind Moue in Charitie, Rest in Proudience, and Turne vpon the Poles of *Truth*.

To passe from Theologicall, and Philosophicall *Truth*, to the *Truth* of ciuill Businesse; It will be acknowledged, euen by those, that practize it not, that cleare and Round dealing, is the Honour of Mans Nature; And that Mixture of Falshood, is like Allay in Coyne of Gold and Siluer; which may make the Metall worke the better, but it embaseth it. For these winding, and crooked courses, are the Goings of the Serpent; which goeth basely vpon the belly, and not vpon the Feet. There is no Vice, that doth so couer a Man with Shame, as to be found false, and perfidious. And therefore *Mountaigny* saith prettily, when he enquired the reason, why the word of the *Lie*, should be such a Disgrace, and such an Odious Charge? Saith he, *If it be well weighed, To say that a man lieth, is as much to say, as that he is braue towards God, and a Coward towards men.* For a *Lie* faces God, and shrinkes from Man. Surely the Wickednesse of Falshood, and Breach of Faith, cannot possibly be so highly expressed, as in that it shall be the last Peale, to call the Iudgements of God, vpon the Generations of Men, It being foretold that when Christ commeth, *He shall not finde Faith vpon the Earth.*

OF STUDIES

Studies serve for Delight, for Ornament, and for Ability. Their Chiefe Vse for Delight, is in Priuatnesse and Retiring; For Ornament, is in Discourse; And for Ability, is in the Iudgement and Disposition of Businesse. For Expert Men can Execute, and perhaps Iudge of particulars, one by one; But the generall Counsels, and the Plots, and Marshalling of Affaires, come best from those that are *Learned.*

To spend too much Time in *Studies*, is Sloth; To vse them too much for Ornament, is Affectation; To make Iudgement wholly by their Rules is the Humour of a Scholler.

They perfect Nature, and are perfected by Experience: For Naturall Abilities, are like Naturall Plants, that need Proyning by *Study*: And *Studies* themselues, doe giue forth Directions too much at Large, except they be bounded in by experience.

Crafty Men Contemne *Studies*; Simple Men Admire them; and Wise Men Vse them: For they teach not their owne Vse; But that is a Wisdome without them, and aboue them, won by Obseruation.

Reade not to Contradict, and Confute; Nor to Beleeue and Take for granted; Nor to Finde Talke and Discourse; But to weigh and Consider.

Some *Bookes* are to be Tasted, Others to be Swallowed, and Some Few to be Chewed and Digested: That is, some *Bookes* are to be read onely in Partes; Others to be read but not Curiously; And some Few to be read wholly, and with Diligence and Attention.

Some *Bookes* also may be read by Deputy, and Extracts made of them by Others: But that would be, onely in the lesse important Arguments, and the Meaner Sort of *Bookes*: else distilled *Bookes*, are like Common distilled Waters, Flashy things.

Reading maketh a Full Man; Conference a Ready Man; And Writing an Exact Man. And therefore, If a Man Write little, he had need haue a Great memory; If he Conferre little, he had need haue a Present Wit; And if he Reade little, he had need haue much Cunning, to seeme to know that, he doth not.

Histories make men Wise; *Poets* Witty; the *Mathematicks* Subtill; *Naturall Philosophy* deepe; *Morall* Graue; *Logick* and *Rhetorick* Able to Contend.

Abeunt studia in Mores. Nay there is no Stond or Impediment in the Wit, but may be wrought out by Fit *Studies*; Like as Diseases of the Body, may haue Appropriate Exercises. Bowling is good for the Stone and Reines; Shooting for the Lungs and Breast; Gentle

Walking for the Stomacke; Riding for the Head; And the like. So if a Mans Wit be Wandring, let him *Study* the *Mathematicks*; For in Demonstrations, if his Wit be called away neuer so little, he must begin again: If his Wit be not Apt to distinguish or find differences, let him *Study* the *Schoolemen*; For they are *Cymini sectores*.

If he be not Apt to beat ouer Matters, and to call vp one Thing, to Proue and Illustrate another, let him *Study* the *Lawyers Cases*: So euery Defect of the Minde, may haue a Speciall Receit.

ABRAHAM COWLEY

(1618–1667)

Abraham Cowley was the son of a wealthy citizen of London, and became a classical scholar at Cambridge. He is better known for his verse than for his prose: nevertheless he represents the transition from the condensed style of Bacon to the easy flowing style of Addison and Steele. But although he was more popular in his own day than he is now, he merits inclusion in any representative collection of essays; and the essay here printed is one of his pleasantest, as well as being probably the best known of his essays. Fame came to him early: he wrote competent, though not great, verse before he was sixteen years old.

OF MYSELF

It is a hard and nice subject for a man to write of himself; it grates his own heart to say anything of disparagement and the reader's ears to hear anything of praise for him. There is no danger from me of offending him in this kind; neither my mind, nor my body, nor my fortune allow me any materials for that vanity. It is sufficient for my own contentment that they have preserved me from being scandalous, or remarkable on the defective side. But besides that, I shall here speak of myself only in relation to the subject of these precedent discourses, and shall be likelier thereby to fall into the contempt than rise up to the estimation of most people. As far as my memory can return back into my

7

past life, before I knew or was capable of guessing what the world, or glories, or business of it were, the natural affections of my soul gave me a secret bent of aversion from them, as some plants are said to turn away from others, by an antipathy imperceptible to themselves and inscrutable to man's understanding. Even when I was a very young boy at school, instead of running about on holidays and playing with my fellows, I was wont to steal from them and walk into the fields, either alone with a book, or with some one companion, if I could find any of the same temper. I was then, too, so much an enemy to all constraint, that my masters could never prevail on me, by any persuasions or encouragements, to learn without book the common rules of grammar, in which they dispensed with me alone, because they found I made a shift to do the usual exercises out of my own reading and observation. That I was then of the same mind as I am now (which I confess I wonder at myself) may appear by the latter end of an ode which I made when I was but thirteen years old, and which was then printed with many other verses. The beginning of it is boyish, but of this part which I here set down, if a very little were corrected, I should hardly now be much ashamed.

IX

This only grant me, that my means may lie
Too low for envy, for contempt too high.
    Some honour I would have,
Not from great deeds, but good alone.
The unknown are better than ill known.
    Rumour can ope the grave;
Acquaintance I would have, but when it depends
Not on the number, but the choice of friends.

X

Books should, not business, entertain the light,
And sleep, as undisturbed as death, the night.
        My house a cottage, more
Than palace, and should fitting be
For all my use, no luxury.
        My garden painted o'er
With Nature's hand, not Art's; and pleasures yield,
Horace might envy in his Sabine field.

XI

Thus would I double my life's fading space,
For he that runs it well twice runs his race.
        And in this true delight,
These unbought sports, this happy state,
I would not fear, nor wish my fate,
        But boldly say each night,
To-morrow let my sun his beams display
Or in clouds hide them—I have lived to-day.

You may see by it I was even then acquainted with
the poets (for the conclusion is taken out of Horace),
and perhaps it was the immature and immoderate love
of them which stamped first, or rather engraved, these
characters in me. They were like letters cut into the
bark of a young tree, which with the tree still grow
proportionably. But how this love came to be produced
in me so early is a hard question. I believe I can tell
the particular little chance that filled my head first with
such chimes of verse as have never since left ringing there.
For I remember when I began to read, and to take some
pleasure in it, there was wont to lie in my mother's

parlour (I know not by what accident, for she herself
never in her life read any book but of devotion), but
there was wont to lie Spenser's works; this I happened
to fall upon, and was infinitely delighted with the stories
of the knights, and giants, and monsters, and brave houses,
which I found everywhere there (though my understanding had little to do with all this); and by degrees
with the tinkling of the rhyme and dance of the numbers,
so that I think I had read him all over before I was
twelve years old, and was thus made a poet immediately. With these affections of mind, and my
heart wholly set upon letters, I went to the university, but was soon torn from thence by that violent
public storm which would suffer nothing to stand where
it did, but rooted up every plant, even from the princely
cedars to me, the hyssop. Yet I had as good fortune as
could have befallen me in such a tempest; for I was
cast by it into the family of one of the best persons, and
into the court of one of the best princesses of the world.
Now though I was here engaged in ways most contrary
to the original design of my life, that is, into much company, and no small business, and into a daily sight of
greatness, both militant and triumphant, for that was the
state then of the English and French Courts; yet all this
was so far from altering my opinion, that it only added
the confirmation of reason to that which was before but
natural inclination. I saw plainly all the paint of that
kind of life, the nearer I came to it; and that beauty
which I did not fall in love with when, for aught I knew,
it was real, was not like to bewitch or entice me when
I saw that it was adulterate. I met with several great
persons, whom I liked very well, but could not perceive
that any part of their greatness was to be liked or de-

sired, no more than I would be glad or content to be in a storm, though I saw many ships which rode safely and bravely in it. A storm would not agree with my stomach, if it did with my courage. Though I was in a crowd of as good company as could be found anywhere, though I was in business of great and honourable trust, though I ate at the best table, and enjoyed the best conveniences for present subsistence that ought to be desired by a man of my condition in banishment and public distresses, yet I could not abstain from renewing my old schoolboy's wish in a copy of verses to the same effect.

> Well then; I now do plainly see,
> This busy world and I shall ne'er agree, etc.

And I never then proposed to myself any other advantage from his Majesty's happy restoration, but the getting into some moderately convenient retreat in the country, which I thought in that case I might easily have compassed, as well as some others, with no greater probabilities or pretences, have arrived to extraordinary fortunes. But I had before written a shrewd prophecy against myself, and I think Apollo inspired me in the truth, though not in the elegance of it.

> Thou, neither great at court nor in the war,
> Nor at th' exchange shalt be, nor at the wrangling bar;
> Content thyself with the small barren praise,
> Which neglected verse does raise, etc.

However, by the failing of the forces which I had expected, I did not quit the design which I had resolved on; I cast myself into it *A corps perdu*, without making capitulations or taking counsel of fortune. But God laughs at a man who says to his soul, " Take thy ease ":

I met presently not only with many little encumbrances
and impediments, but with so much sickness (a new
misfortune to me) as would have spoiled the happiness
of an emperor as well as mine. Yet I do neither repent
nor alter my course. *Non ego perfidum dixi sacramentum.*
Nothing shall separate me from a mistress which I have
loved so long, and have now at last married, though she
neither has brought me a rich portion, nor lived yet so
quietly with me as I hoped from her.

> —— *Nec vos, dulcissima mundi*
> *Nomina, vos Musæ, libertas, otia, libri,*
> *Hortique sylvæque anima remanente relinquam.*

> Nor by me e'er shall you,
> You of all names the sweetest, and the best,
> You Muses, books, and liberty, and rest;
> You gardens, fields, and woods forsaken be,
> As long as life itself forsakes not me.

But this is a very petty ejaculation. Because I have
concluded all the other chapters with a copy of verses,
I will maintain the humour to the last.

MARTIAL, LIB. 10, EP. 47

Vitam quæ faciunt beatiorem, etc.

Since, dearest friend, 'tis your desire to see
A true receipt of happiness from me;
These are the chief ingredients, if not all:
Take an estate neither too great nor small,
Which *quantum sufficit* the doctors call;
Let this estate from parents' care descend:
The getting it too much of life does spend.

Take such a ground, whose gratitude may be
A fair encouragement for industry.
Let constant fires the winter's fury tame,
And let thy kitchens be a vestal flame.
Thee to the town let never suit at law,
And rarely, very rarely, business draw.
Thy active mind in equal temper keep,
In undisturbed peace, yet not in sleep.
Let exercise a vigorous health maintain,
Without which all the composition's vain.
In the same weight prudence and innocence take
Ana of each does the just mixture make.
But a few friendships wear, and let them be
By Nature and by Fortune fit for thee.
Instead of art and luxury in food,
Let mirth and freedom make thy table good.
If any cares into thy daytime creep,
At night, without wines, opium, let them sleep.
Let rest, which Nature does to darkness wed,
And not lust, recommend to thee thy bed,
Be satisfied, and pleased with what thou art;
Act cheerfully and well the allotted part.
Enjoy the present hour, be thankful for the past,
And neither fear, nor wish the approaches of the last.

MARTIAL, LIB. 10, EP. 96

Me, who have lived so long among the great,
You wonder to hear talk of a retreat:
And a retreat so distant, as may show
No thoughts of a return when once I go.
Give me a country, how remote so e'er,
Where happiness a moderate rate does bear,

Where poverty itself in plenty flows
And all the solid use of riches knows.
The ground about the house maintains it there,
The house maintains the ground about it here.
Here even hunger's dear, and a full board
Devours the vital substance of the lord.
The land itself does there the feast bestow,
The land itself must here to market go.
Three or four suits one winter here does waste,
One suit does there three or four winters last.
Here every frugal man must oft be cold,
And little lukewarm fires are to you sold.
There fire's an element as cheap and free
Almost as any of the other three.
Stay you then here, and live among the great,
Attend their sports, and at their tables eat.
When all the bounties here of men you score,
The Place's bounty there, shall give me more.

SIR RICHARD STEELE

(1672–1729)

Steele was the lifelong friend of Addison; but in character the two men could scarcely have been more unlike. Steele was a blustering, reckless soldier, lacking the care and precision of Addison, but possessing a strength that is missing from Addison's more careful prose. It was Steele who founded the *Tatler*, and who originally suggested the idea of the Spectator Club; but the credit of carrying out the idea must be divided between the two friends. Each of them possessed certain qualities which the other lacked; together they made an almost ideal combination.

A RAMBLE FROM RICHMOND TO LONDON

Sine me, vacivum tempus ne quod dem mihi Laboris.

Terence.

It is an inexpressible Pleasure to know a little of the World, and be of no Character or Significancy in it.

To be ever unconcerned, and ever looking on new Objects with an endless Curiosity, is a Delight known only to those who are turned for Speculation: Nay, they who enjoy it, must value things only as they are the Objects of Speculation, without drawing any worldly Advantage to themselves from them, but just as they are what contribute to their Amusement, or the Improvement of the Mind. I lay one Night last Week at *Richmond*; and being restless, not out of Dissatisfaction, but a certain busie Inclination one sometimes has, I arose at Four in the Morning, and took Boat for *London*, with a Resolution to rove by Boat and Coach for the next Four and twenty Hours, till the many different Objects I must needs meet with should tire my Imagination, and give me an Inclination to a Repose more profound than I was at that time capable of. I beg People's Pardon for an odd Humour I am guilty of, and was often that Day, which is saluting any Person whom I like, whether I know him or not. This is a Particularity would be tolerated in me, if they considered that the greatest Pleasure I know I receive at my Eyes, and that I am obliged to an agreeable Person for coming abroad into my View, as another is for a Visit of Conversation at their own Houses.

The Hours of the Day and Night are taken up in the Cities of *London* and *Westminster* by People as different from each other as those who are Born in different Centuries. Men of Six-a-Clock give way to those of Nine, they of Nine to the Generation of Twelve, and they of Twelve disappear, and make Room for the fashionable World, who have made Two-a-Clock the Noon of the Day.

When we first put off from Shoar, we soon fell in with a Fleet of Gardiners bound for the several Market-Ports of *London*; and it was the most pleasing Scene imaginable to see the Chearfulness with which those industrious People ply'd their Way to a certain Sale of their Goods. The Banks on each Side are as well Peopled, and beautified with as agreeable Plantations, as any Spot on the Earth; but the *Thames* it self, loaded with the Product of each Shoar, added very much to the Landskip. It was very easie to observe by their Sailing, and the Counte-

nances of the ruddy Virgins, who were Supercargos, the
Parts of the Town to which they were bound. There
was an Air in the Purveyors for *Covent-Garden*, who
frequently converse with Morning Rakes, very unlike
the seemly Sobriety of those bound for *Stocks-Market*.

Nothing remarkable happened in our Voyage: but I
landed with Ten Sail of Apricock Boats at *Strand-
Bridge*, after having put in at *Nine-Elmes*, and taken in
Melons, consigned by Mr. *Cuffe* of that Place, to *Sarah
Sewell* and Company, at their Stall in *Covent-Garden*.
We arrived at *Strand-Bridge* at Six of the Clock, and
were unloading; when the Hackney-Coachmen of the
foregoing Night took their Leave of each other at the
Dark-House, to go to Bed before the Day was too far
spent. Chimney-Sweepers pass'd by us as we made up
to the Market, and some Raillery happened between one
of the Fruit-Wenches and those black Men, about the
Devil and *Eve*, with Allusion to their several Professions.
I could not believe any Place more entertaining than
Covent-Garden; where I strolled from one Fruit-shop to
another, with Crowds of agreeable young Women around
me, who were purchasing Fruit for their respective
Families. It was almost Eight of the Clock before I could
leave that Variety of Objects. I took Coach and followed
a young Lady, who tripped into another just before me,
attended by her Maid. I saw immediately she was of the
Family of the *Vainloves*. There are a Sett of these, who
of all things affect the Play of *Blindman's-Buff*, and leading
Men into Love for they know not whom, who are fled
they know not where. This sort of Woman is usually a
janty Slattern; she hangs on her Cloaths, plays her
Head, varies her Posture, and changes place incessantly,
and all with an Appearance of striving at the same time

to hide her self, and yet give you to understand she is in Humour to laugh at you. You must have often seen the Coachmen make Signs with their Fingers as they drive by each other, to intimate how much they have got that Day. They can carry on that Language to give Intelligence where they are driving. In an Instant my Coachman took the Wink to pursue, and the Lady's Driver gave the Hint that he was going through *Long-Acre* towards St. *James's*: while he whipp'd up *James-Street*, we drove for *King Street*, to save the Pass at St. *Martin's Lane*. The Coachmen took care to meet, justle, and threaten each other for Way, and be intangled at the End of *Newport-Street* and *Long-Acre*. The Fright, you must believe, brought down the Lady's Coach Door, and obliged her, with her Mask off, to enquire into the Bustle, when she sees the Man she would avoid. The Tackle of the Coach-Window is so bad she cannot draw it up again, and she drives on sometimes wholly discovered, and sometimes half-escaped, according to the Accident of Carriages in her Way. One of these Ladies keeps her Seat in a Hackney-Coach as well as the best Rider does on a managed Horse. The laced Shooe on her Left Foot, with a careless Gesture, just appearing on the opposite Cushion, held her both firm, and in a proper Attitude to receive the next Jolt.

As she was an excellent Coach-Woman, many were the Glances at each other which we had for an Hour and an Half in all Parts of the Town by the Skill of our Drivers; till at last my Lady was conveniently lost with Notice from her Coachman to ours to make off, and he should hear where she went. This Chace was now at an End, and the Fellow who drove her came to us, and discovered that he was ordered to come again in an Hour, for that she was a Silk-Worm. I was surprized with this Phrase, but found it was a Cant among the Hackney Fraternity for their best Customers, Women who ramble twice or thrice a Week from Shop to Shop, to turn over all the Goods in Town without buying any thing. The Silk-Worms are, it seems, indulged by the Tradesmen; for tho' they never buy, they are ever talking of new Silks, Laces and Ribbands, and serve the Owners in getting them Customers, as their common Dunners do in making them pay.

The Day of People of Fashion began now to break, and Carts and Hacks were mingled with Equipages of Show and Vanity; when I resolved to walk it out of Cheapness; but my unhappy Curiosity is such, that I find it always my Interest to take Coach, for some odd Adventure among Beggars, Ballad-Singers, or the like, detains and throws me into Expence. It happened so immediately; for at the Corner of *Warwick-Street*, as I was listening to a new Ballad, a ragged Rascal, a Beggar who knew me, came up to me, and began to turn the Eyes of the good Company upon me, by telling me he was extream Poor, and should die in the Streets for want of Drink, except I immediately would have the Charity to give him Six-pence to go into the next Ale-House and save his life. He urged, with a melancholy Face, that all his Family had died of Thirst. All the Mob have Humour, and two or three began to take the Jest; by which Mr. *Sturdy* carried his Point, and let me sneak off to a Coach. As I drove along it was a pleasing Reflection to see the World so prettily chequered since I left *Richmond*, and the Scene still filling with Children of a new Hour. This Satisfaction encreased as I moved towards the City: and gay Signs, well disposed Streets, magnificent publick Structures, and Wealthy Shops, adorned with contented Faces, made the Joy still rising till we came into the Centre of the City, and Centre of the World of Trade, the *Exchange* of *London*. As other Men in the Crowds about me were pleased with their Hopes and Bargains, I found my Account in observing them, in Attention to their several Interests. I, indeed, looked upon my self as the richest Man that walked the *Exchange* that Day; for my Benevolence made me share the Gains of every bargain that was made. It was not the least of the Satisfactions in my Survey, to go up Stairs, and pass the Shops of agreeable Females; to observe so many pretty Hands busie in the Foldings of Ribbands, and the utmost Eagerness of agreeable Faces in the Sale of Patches, Pins and Wires, on each Side the Counters, was an Amusement, in which I should longer have indulged my self, had not the dear Creatures called to me to ask what I wanted, when I could not answer, only *To look at you.* I went to one of the Windows which opened to the Area below, where all the several Voices lost their Distinction, and rose up in a confused Humming; which created in me a Reflection that could not come into the Mind of any but of one a little studious; for I said to my self, with a kind of Punn in thought, *What Nonsense is all the Hurry of this World to those who are above it?* In these, or not much wiser Thoughts, I had like to have lost my Place at the Chop-House; where every Man, according to the natural Bashfulness or Sullenness of our Nation, eats in a publick Room a Mess of Broth, or Chop of Meat, in dumb Silence, as if they had no Pretence to speak to each other on the Foot of being Men, except they were of each other's Acquaintance.

I went afterwards to *Robin's* and saw People who had dined with me at the Five-Penny Ordinary just before, give Bills for the Value of large Estates; and could not but behold with great Pleasure, Property lodged in, and transferred in a Moment from such as would never be Masters of half as much as is seemingly in them, and given from them every Day they live. But before Five in the Afternoon I left the City, came to my common Scene of *Covent-Garden*, and passed the Evening at *Will's*, in attending the Discourses of several Sets of People, who relieved each other within my Hearing on the Subjects of Cards, Dice, Love, Learning and Politicks. The last Subject kept me till I heard the Streets in the Possession of the Bell-man, who had now the World to himself, and cryed, *Past Two of Clock*. This rous'd me from my Seat, and I went to my Lodging, led by a Light, whom I put into the Discourse of his private Oeconomy, and made him give me an Account of the Charge, Hazard, Profit and Loss of a Family that depended upon a Link, with a Design to end my trivial Day with the Generosity of Six-pence, instead of a third Part of that Sum. When I came to my Chambers I writ down these Minutes; but was at a Loss what Instruction I should propose to my Reader from the Enumeration of so many Insignificant Matters and Occurrences; and I thought it of great Use, if they could learn with me to keep their minds open to Gratification, and ready to receive it from any thing it meets with. This one Circumstance will make every Face you see give you the Satisfaction you now take in beholding that of a Friend; will make every Object a pleasing one; will make all the Good which arrives to any Man, an Encrease of Happiness to your self.

THE SPECTATOR CLUB

. . . *Haec alii sex*
Vel plures uno conclamant ore

Juvenal.

The first of our Society is a Gentleman of *Worcester-shire*, of antient Descent, a Baronet, his Name Sir ROGER DE COVERLEY. His great Grandfather was Inventor of that famous Country-Dance which is call'd after him. All who know that Shire are very well acquainted with the Parts and Merits of Sir ROGER. He is a Gentleman that is very singular in his Behaviour, but his Singularities proceed from his good Sense, and are Contradictions to the Manners of the World, only as he thinks the World is in the wrong. However, this Humour creates him no Enemies, for he does nothing with Sourness or Obstinacy; and his being unconfined to Modes and Forms, makes him but the readier and more capable to please and oblige all who know him. When he is in town he lives in *Soho-Square*: It is said, he keeps himself a Batchelor by reason he was crossed in Love, by a perverse beautiful Widow of the next County to him. Before this Disappointment, Sir ROGER was what you call a fine Gentleman, had often supped with my Lord *Rochester* and Sir *George Etherege*, fought a Duel upon his first coming to Town, and kick'd Bully *Dawson* in a publick Coffee-house for calling him Youngster. But being ill used by the above-mentioned Widow, he was very serious for a Year and a half; and though, his Temper being naturally jovial, he at last got over it, he grew careless of himself, and never dressed afterwards; he continues to wear a Coat and Doublet of the same Cut that were in Fashion at the Time of his Repulse, which, in his merry Humours, he tells us, has been in and out twelve Times since he first wore it. He is now in his Fifty sixth Year, cheerful, gay, and hearty, keeps a good House both in Town and Country; a great Lover of Mankind; but there is such a mirthful Cast in his Behaviour, that he is rather beloved than esteemed: His Tenants grow rich, his Servants look satisfied, all the young Women profess Love to him, and the young Men are glad of his Company: When he comes into a House he calls the Servants by their Names, and talks all the way up Stairs to a Visit. I must not omit that Sir ROGER is a Justice of the *Quorum*; that he fills the chair at a Quarter-Session with great Abilities, and three Months ago gain'd universal Applause by explaining a Passage in the Game-Act.

The Gentleman next in Esteem and Authority among us, is another Batchelor, who is a Member of the *Inner Temple*; a Man of great Probity, Wit, and Understanding; but he has chosen his Place of Residence rather to obey the Direction of an old humoursom Father, than in pursuit of his own Inclinations. He was placed there to study the Laws of the Land, and is the most learned of any of the House in those of the Stage. *Aristotle* and *Longinus* are much better understood by him than *Littleton* or *Cooke*. The Father sends up every Post Questions relating to Marriage-Articles, Leases, and Tenures, in the Neighbourhood; all which Questions he agrees with an Attorney to answer and take care of in the Lump: He is studying the Passions themselves, when he should be enquiring into the Debates among Men which arise from them. He knows the Argument of each of the Orations of *Demosthenes* and *Tully*, but not one Case in the Reports of our own Courts. No one ever took him for a Fool, but none, except his intimate Friends, know he has a great deal of Wit. This Turn makes him at once both disinterested and agreeable: As few of his Thoughts are drawn from Business, they are most of them fit for Conversation. His Taste of Books is a little too just for the Age he lives in; he has read all, but approves of very few. His Familiarity with the Customs, Manners, Actions, and Writings of the Antients, makes him a very delicate Observer of what occurs to him in the present World. He is an excellent Critick, and the Time of the Play is his Hour of Business; exactly at five he passes thro' *New-Inn*, crosses thro' *Russel-Court*, and takes a turn at *Will's* 'till the play begins; he has his Shooes rubbed and his Perriwig powder'd at the Barber's as you go into the *Rose*. It is for the Good of the Audience when he is at a Play, for the Actors have an Ambition to please him.

The Person of next Consideration is Sir ANDREW FREEPORT, a Merchant of great Eminence in the City of *London*. A Person of indefatigable Industry, strong Reason, and great Experience. His Notions of Trade are noble and generous, and (as every rich Man has usually some sly Way of Jesting, which would make no great Figure were he not a rich Man) he calls the Sea the *British Common*. He is acquainted with Commerce in all its Parts, and will tell you that it is a stupid and barbarous Way to extend Dominion by Arms; for true Power is to be got by Arts and Industry. He will often argue, that if this Part of our Trade were well cultivated, we should gain from one Nation; and if another, from another. I have heard him prove, that Diligence makes more lasting Acquisitions than Valour, and that Sloth has ruined more Nations than the Sword. He abounds in several frugal Maxims, among which the greatest Favourite is " A Penny saved is a Penny got ". A General Trader of good Sense, is pleasanter company than a general Scholar; and Sir ANDREW having a natural unaffected Eloquence, the Perspicuity of his Discourse gives the same Pleasure that Wit would in another man. He has made his Fortunes himself; and says that *England* may be richer than other Kingdoms, by as plain Methods as he himself is richer than other Men; tho' at the same Time I can say this of him, that there is not a point in the Compass but blows home a Ship in which he is an Owner.

Next to Sir ANDREW in the Club-room sits Captain SENTRY, a Gentleman of great Courage, good Understanding, but invincible Modesty. He is one of those that deserve very well, but are very awkward at putting their Talents within the Observation of such as should take Notice of them. He was some Years a Captain, and behaved himself with great Gallantry in several Engagements, and at several Sieges; but having a small Estate of his own, and being next Heir to Sir ROGER, he has quitted a Way of Life in which no Man can rise suitably to his Merit, who is not something of a Courtier as well as a Soldier. I have heard him often lament, that in a Profession where Merit is placed in so conspicuous a View, Impudence should get the better of Modesty. When he has talked to this Purpose I never heard him make a sour Expression, but frankly confess that he left the World, because he was not fit for it. A strict Honesty and an even regular Behaviour, are in themselves Obstacles to him that must press through Crowds, who endeavour at the same End with himself, the Favour of a Commander. He will however in his Way of Talk excuse Generals, for nor disposing according to Mens Desert, or enquiring into it: For, says he, that great Man who has a Mind to help me, has as many to break through to come at me, as I have to come at him: Therefore he will conclude, that the Man who would make a Figure, especially in a military Way, must get over all false Modesty, and assist his Patron against the Importunity of other Pretenders, by a proper Assurance in his own Vindication. He says it is a Civil Cowardice to be backward in asserting what you ought to expect, as it is a military Fear to be slow in attacking when it is your Duty. With this Candour does the Gentleman speak of himself and others. The same Frankness runs through all his Conversation. The military Part of his Life has furnish'd him with many Adventures, in the Relation of which he is very agreeable to the Company; for he is never over-bearing, though accustomed to command Men in the utmost Degree below him; nor ever too obsequious, from an Habit of obeying Men highly above him.

But that our Society may not appear a Set of Humourists unacquainted with the Gallantries and Pleasures of the Age, we have among us the gallant WILL HONEYCOMB, a Gentleman who according to his Years should be in the Decline of his Life, but having ever been very careful of his Person, and always had a very easie Fortune, Time has made but very little Impression, either by Wrinkles on his Forehead, or Traces in his Brain. His Person is well turn'd, of a good Height. He is very ready at that sort of Discourse with which Men usually entertain Women. He has all his Life dressed very well, and remembers Habits as others do Men. He can smile when one speaks to him, and laughs easily.

He knows the History of every Mode, and can inform you from which of the *French* King's Wenches our Wives and Daughters had this Manner of curling their Hair, that way of placing their Hoods, and whose Vanity to shew her Foot made that Part of the Dress so short in such a Year. In a word, all his Conversation and Knowledge has been in the female World: As other Men of his Age will take Notice to you what such a Minister said upon such and such an Occasion, he will tell you when the Duke of *Monmouth* danced at Court such a Woman was then smitten, another was taken with him at the Head of his Troop in the *Park*. In all these important Relations, he has ever about the same Time received a kind Glance or a Blow of a Fan from some celebrated Beauty, Mother of the Present Lord such-a-one. This way of Talking of his very much enlivens the Conversation among us of a more sedate Turn; and I find there is not one of the Company, but my self, who rarely speak at all, but speaks of him as of that Sort of Man, who is usually called a well-bred fine Gentleman. To conclude his Character, where Women are not concern'd, he is an honest worthy Man.

I cannot tell whether I am to account him whom I am next to speak of, as one of our Company; for he visits us but seldom, but when he does it adds to every Man else a new Enjoyment of himself. He is a Clergyman, a very philosophick Man, of general Learning, great Sanctity of Life, and the most exact good Breeding. He has the Misfortune to be of a very weak Constitution, and consequently cannot accept of such Cares and Business as Preferments in his Function would oblige him to: He is therefore among Divines what a Chamber-Counsellor is among Lawyers. The Probity of his Mind, and the Integrity of his Life, create him Followers, as being eloquent or loud advances others. He seldom introduces the Subject he speaks upon; but we are so far gone in Years, that he observes, when he is among us, an Earnestness to have him fall on some divine Topick, which he always treats with much Authority, as one who has no Interests in this World, as one who is hastening to the Object of all his Wishes, and conceives Hope from his Decays and Infirmities. These are my ordinary Companions.

SIR ROGER DE COVERLEY'S PORTRAIT GALLERY

. . . . *Abnormis sapiens*

Horace.

I was this Morning walking in the Gallery, when Sir ROGER enter'd at the end opposite to me, and advancing towards me, said, he was glad to meet me among his Relations the DE COVERLEYS, and hoped I liked the Conversation of so much good Company, who were as silent as my self. I knew he alluded to the Pictures, and as he is a Gentleman who does not a little value himself upon his ancient Descent, I expected he would give me some Account of them. We were now arrived at the upper End of the Gallery, when the Knight faced towards one of the Pictures, and as we stood before it, he entered into the Matter, after his blunt way of saying things, as they occur to his Imagination, without regular Introduction, or Care to preserve the Appearance of Chain of Thought.

" It is," said he, " worth while to consider the Force of Dress; and how the Persons of one Age differ from those of another, merely by that only. One may observe also that the General Fashion of one Age has been follow'd by one particular Set of People in another, and by them preserved from one Generation to another. Thus the vast Jetting Coat and small Bonnet, which was the Habit in *Harry* the Seventh's time, is kept on in the Yeomen of the Guard; not without a good and Politick View, because they look a Foot taller, and a Foot and an half broader: Besides, that the Cap leaves the Face expanded, and consequently more Terrible, and fitter to stand at the Entrance of Palaces.

" This Predecessor of ours, you see, is dressed after this Manner, and his Cheeks would be no larger than mine were he in a Hat as I am. He was the last Man that won a Prize in the Tilt-Yard (which is now a Common Street before *Whitehall*). You see the broken Lance that lyes there by his right Foot; he shivered that Lance of his Adversary all to pieces; and bearing himself, look you, Sir, in this manner, at the same time he came within the Target of the Gentleman who rode again him, and taking him with incredible Force before him on the Pummel of his Saddle, he in that manner rid the Turnament over, with an Air that shewed he did it rather to perform the Rule of the Lists, than Expose his Enemy; however, it appeared he knew how to make use of a Victory, and with a gentle Trot he marched up to a Gallery where their Mistress sat (for they were Rivals) and let him down with laudable courtesy and pardonable Indolence. I don't know but it might be exactly where the Coffee-house is now.

" You are to know this my Ancestor was not only of a

military Genius but fit also for the Arts of Peace, for he play'd on the Base-Viol as well as any Gentleman at Court; you see where his Viol hangs by his Basket-hilt Sword. The Action at the Tilt-Yard you may be sure won the Fair Lady, who was a Maid of Honour, and the greatest Beauty of her time; here she stands, the next Picture. You see, Sir, my Great Great Great Grand-mother has on the new-fashioned Petticoat, except that the Modern is gathered at the Waste; my Grandmother appears as if she stood in a large Drum, whereas the Ladies now walk as if they were in a Go-Cart. For all this Lady was bred at Court, she became an Excellent Country-Wife, she brought ten Children, and when I shew you the Library, you shall see in her own hand (allowing for the Difference of the Language) the best Receipt now in *England* both for an Hasty-Pudding and a Whitepot.

"If you please to fall back a little, because it is neces-sary to look at the three next Pictures at one View; these are three Sisters. She on the right Hand, who is so very beautiful, dyed a Maid; the next to her, still handsomer, had the same Fate, against her Will; this homely thing in the middle had both their Portions added to her own, and was Stolen by a neighbouring Gentleman, a Man of Stratagem and Resolution, for he poisoned three Mastiffs to come at her, and knocked down two Dear-stealers in carrying her off. Misfor-tunes happen in all Families; The Theft of this Romp and so much Money, was no great matter to our Estate. But the next Heir that possessed it was this soft Gentle-man, whom you see there: Observe the small Buttons, the little Boots, the Laces, the Slashes about his Cloaths, and above all the Posture he is drawn in, (which to be sure was his own chusing); you see he sits with one Hand on a Desk writing, and looking as it were another way, like an easie Writer, or a Sonneteer: He was one of those that had too much Wit to know how to live in the World; he was a Man of no Justice, but great good Manners; he ruined every body that had any thing to do with him, but never said a rude thing in his Life; the most indolent Person in the World, he would sign a Deed that passed away half his Estate with his Gloves on, but would not put on his Hat before a Lady if it were to save his Country. He is said to be the first that made Love by squeezing the Hand. He left the Estate with ten thousand Pounds Debt upon it, but however by all Hands I have been informed that he was every way the finest Gentleman in the World. That Debt lay heavy on our House for one Generation, but it was retrieved by a Gift from that Honest Man you see there, a Citizen of our Name, but nothing at all a-kin to us. I know Sir ANDREW FREEPORT has said behind my Back, that this Man was descended from one of the ten Children of the Maid of Honour I shewed you above. But it was never made out; we winked at the thing indeed, because Mony was wanting at that time."

Here I saw my Friend a little embarrassed, and turned my Face to the next Portraiture.

Sir ROGER went on with his Account of the Gallery in the following manner. " This Man " (pointing to him I look'd at) " I take to be the Honour of our House. Sir HUMPHREY DE COVERLEY; he was in his Dealings as punctual as a Tradesman, and as generous as a Gentleman. He would have thought himself as much undone by breaking his Word, as if it were to be followed by Bankruptcy. He served his Country as Knight of this

Shire to his dying Day: He found it no easie matter to maintain an Integrity in his Words and Actions, even in things that regarded the Offices which were incumbent upon him, in the care of his own Affairs and Relations of Life, and therefore dreaded (tho' he had great Talents) to go into Employments of State, where he must be exposed to the Snares of Ambition. Innocence of Life and great Ability were the distinguishing Parts of his Character; the latter, he had often observed, had led to the Destruction of the former, and used frequently to lament that Great and Good had not the same Signification. He was an excellent Husbandman, but had resolved not to exceed such a degree of Wealth; all above it he bestowed in secret Bounties many Years after the Sum he aimed at for his own use was attained. Yet he did not slacken his Industry, but to a decent old Age spent the Life and Fortune which was superfluous to himself, in the Service of his Friends and Neighbours."

Here we were called to Dinner, and Sir ROGER ended the Discourse of this Gentleman, by telling me, as we followed the Servant, that this his Ancestor was a Brave Man, and narrowly escaped being killed in the Civil Wars; " for," said he, " he was sent out of the Field upon a private Message the Day before the Battle of *Worcester*." The Whim of narrowly escaping, by having been within a Day of Danger; with other Matters abovementioned, mixed with good Sense, left me at a Loss whether I was more delighted with my Friend's Wisdom or Simplicity.

JOSEPH ADDISON

(1672–1719)

Addison, one of the gentlest of men, early became a scholar of note. Along with Steele, he developed the English essay form in the direction indicated by Cowley, and devoted himself to the production of short essays suitable for publication in the periodicals which began to be popular in the early eighteenth century — the *Tatler* and the *Spectator*. His style is polished, easy, and pleasant, and his English was regarded as a model of perfection for two hundred years. His influence on the English essay is enormous; and the continuity of such a series as the Sir Roger de Coverley essays also strongly influenced the English novel.

SIR ROGER AND WILL WIMBLE

Gratis anhelans, multo agendo nihil agens

Phaedrus.

As I was Yesterday Morning walking with Sir ROGER before his House, a Country-Fellow brought him a huge Fish, which, he told him, Mr. *William Wimble* had caught that very Morning; and that he presented it, with his Service, to him, and intended to come and dine with him. At the same Time he delivered a Letter, which my Friend read to me as soon as the Messenger left him.

" *Sir* ROGER,

    I Desire you to accept of a Jack, which is the best I have caught this Season. I intend to come and stay with you a Week, and see how the Perch bite in the *Black River*. I observed, with some Concern, the last Time I saw you upon the Bowling-Green, that your Whip wanted a Lash to it: I will bring half a Dozen with me that I twisted last Week, which I hope will serve you all the Time you are in the Country. I have not been out of the Saddle for six Days last past, having been at *Eaton* with Sir *John's* eldest Son. He takes to his Learning hugely.

> *I am,*
>> *Sir,*
>>> *Your Humble Servant,*
>>>> Will Wimble."

This extraordinary Letter, and Message that accompanied it, made me very curious to know the Character and Quality of the Gentleman who sent them; which I found to be as follows; *Will Wimble* is younger Brother to a Baronet, and descended of the ancient Family of the *Wimbles*. He is now between Forty and Fifty; but being bred to no Business and born to no Estate, he generally lives with his elder Brother as Superintendent of his Game. He hunts a Pack of Dogs better than any Man in the Country, and is very famous for finding out a Hare. He is extremely well versed in all the little Handicrafts of an idle Man: He makes a *May*-fly to a Miracle; and furnishes the whole Country with Angle-Rods. As he is a good-natur'd officious Fellow, and very much esteemed upon Account of his Family, he is a welcome Guest at every House, and keeps up a good Correspondence among all the Gentlemen about him. He carries a Tulip-Root in his Pocket from one to another, or exchanges a Puppy between a couple of Friends that live perhaps in the opposite Sides of the County. *Will.* is a particular Favourite of all the young Heirs, whom he frequently obliges with a Net that he has weaved, or a Setting-dog that he has *made* himself: He now and then presents a Pair of Garters of his own Knitting to their Mothers or Sisters; and raises a great deal of Mirth among them, by enquiring as often as he meets them *how they wear?* These Gentleman-like Manufactures and obliging little Humours, make *Will.* the Darling of the Country.

Sir ROGER was proceeding in the Character of him, when he saw him make up to us, with two or three Hazletwigs in his Hand that he had cut in Sir ROGER's Woods, as he came through them, in his Way to the House. I was very much pleased to observe on one Side the hearty and sincere welcome with which Sir ROGER received him, and on the other the secret Joy which his Guest discovered at Sight of the good old Knight. After the first Salutes were over, *Will.* desired Sir ROGER to lend him one of his Servants to carry a Set of Shuttlecocks he had with him in a little Box to a Lady that liv'd about a Mile off, to whom it seems he had promised such a Present for above this half Year. Sir ROGER's Back was no sooner turn'd, but honest *Will.* began to tell me of a large Cock-Pheasant that he had sprung in one of the neighbouring Woods, with two or three other Adventures of the same Nature. Odd and uncommon Characters are the Game that I look for, and most delight in; for which Reason I was as much pleased with the Novelty of the Person that talked to me, as he could be for his Life with the springing of a Pheasant, and therefore listned to him with more than ordinary Attention.

In the Midst of his Discourse the Bell rung to Dinner,

where the Gentleman I have been speaking of had the
Pleasure of seeing the huge Jack, he had caught, served
up for the first Dish in a most sumptuous Manner.
Upon our sitting down to it he gave us a long Account
how he had hooked it, played with it, foiled it, and at
length drew it out upon the Bank, with several other
Particulars that lasted all the first Course. A Dish of
Wild-fowl that came afterwards furnished Conversation
for the rest of the Dinner, which concluded with a late
invention of *Will.'s* for improving the Quail Pipe.

Upon withdrawing into my Room after Dinner, I was
secretly touched with Compassion towards the honest
Gentleman that had dined with us; and could not but
consider with a great deal of Concern, how so good an
Heart and such busy Hands were wholly employed in
Trifles; that so much Humanity should be so little
beneficial to others, and so much Industry so little
advantageous to himself. The same Temper of Mind
and Application to Affairs might have recommended
him to the publick Esteem, and have raised his Fortune
in another Station of Life. What Good to his Country
or himself might not a Trader or Merchant have done
with such useful tho' ordinary Qualifications?

Will. Wimble's is the Case of many a younger Brother
of a great Family, who had rather see their Children
starve like Gentlemen, that thrive in a Trade or Profession that is beneath their Quality. This Humour
fills several Parts of *Europe* with Pride and Beggary. It
is the Happiness of a trading Nation, like ours, that the
younger Sons, tho' uncapable of any liberal Art or Profession, may be placed in such a Way of Life, as may
perhaps enable them to vie with the best of their Family:
Accordingly we find several Citizens that were launched

into the World with narrow Fortunes, rising by an honest
Industry to greater Estates than those of their elder
Brothers. It is not improbable but *Will.* was formerly
tried at Divinity, Law, or Physick; and that finding his
Genius did not lie that Way, his Parents gave him up at
length to his own Inventions: But certainly, however
improper he might have been for Studies of a higher
Nature, he was perfectly well turned for the Occupations
of Trade and Commerce. As I think this is a Point
which cannot be too much inculcated, I shall desire my
Reader to compare what I have here written with what
I have said in my Twenty first Speculation.

THE AUTOBIOGRAPHY OF A SHILLING

Per varios casus, per tot discrimina rerum,
Tendimus . . .

Virgil.

I was last Night visited by a Friend of mine who has
an inexhaustible Fund of Discourse, and never fails to
entertain his Company with a Variety of Thoughts and
Hints that are altogether new and uncommon. Whether
it were in Complaisance to my Way of Living, or his real
Opinion, he advanced the following Paradox, That it
required much greater Talents to fill up and become a
retired Life, than a Life of Business. Upon this Occasion he rallied very agreeably the busy Men of the Age,
who only valued themselves for being in Motion, and
passing thro' a Series of trifling and insignificant Actions.
In the Heat of his Discourse, seeing a Piece of Money
lying on my Table, I defy (says he) any of these active

Persons to produce half the Adventures that this Twelvepenny Piece has been engaged in, were it possible for him to give us an Account of his Life.

My Friend's Talk made so odd an Impression upon my Mind, that soon after I was a-Bed I fell insensibly into a most unaccountable *Reverie*, that had neither Moral nor Design in it, and cannot be so properly called a Dream as a Delirium.

Methought the Shilling that lay upon the Table reared it self upon its Edge, and turning the Face towards me, opened its Mouth, and in a soft Silver Sound gave me the following Account of his Life and Adventures:

I was born, says he, on the Side of a Mountain, near a little Village of *Peru*, and made a Voyage to *England* in an Ingot, under the Convoy of Sir *Francis Drake*. I was, soon after my Arrival, taken out of my *Indian* Habit, refined, naturalized, and put into the *British* Mode, with the Face of Queen *Elizabeth* on one Side, and the Arms of the Country on the other. Being thus equipped, I found in me a wonderful Inclination to ramble, and visit all the Parts of the new World into which I was brought. The People very much favoured my natural Disposition, and shifted me so fast from Hand to Hand, that before I was five Years old I had travelled into almost every Corner of the Nation. But in the beginning of my sixth Year, to my unspeakable Grief, I fell into the Hands of a miserable old Fellow, who clapped me into an Iron Chest, where I found five-hundred more of my own Quality who lay under the same Confinement. The only Relief we had, was to be taken out and counted over in the fresh Air every Morning and Evening. After an Imprisonment of several Years we heard some Body knocking at our Chest, and breaking it open with an

Hammer. This we found was the old Man's Heir, who, as his Father lay a dying, was so good as to come to our Release: He separated us that very Day. What was the Fate of my Companions I know not: As for my self, I was sent to the Apothecary's Shop for a Pint of Sack. The Apothecary gave me to an Herb-Woman, the Herb-Woman to a Butcher, the Butcher to a Brewer, and the Brewer to his Wife, who made a present of me to a Non-conformist Preacher. After this manner I made my Way merrily thro' the World; for, as I told you before, we Shillings love nothing so much as Travelling. I sometimes fetched in a Shoulder of Mutton, sometimes a Play-Book, and often had the Satisfaction to treat a Templar at a Twelve-penny Ordinary, or carry him with three Friends to *Westminster Hall.*

In the midst of this pleasant Progress which I made from Place to Place, I was arrested by a superstitious old Woman, who shut me up in a greasy Purse, in pursuance of a foolish Saying, that while she kept a Queen *Elizabeth's* Shilling about her she should never be without Money. I continued here a close Prisoner for many Months, till at last I was exchanged for eight and forty Farthings.

I thus rambled from Pocket to Pocket till the Beginning of the Civil Wars, when (to my Shame be it spoken) I was employed in raising Soldiers against the King: For being of a very tempting Breadth, a Serjeant made use of me to inveigle Country Fellows, and lift them in the Service of the Parliament.

As soon as he had made one Man sure, his Way was to oblige him to take a Shilling of a more homely Figure, and then practise the same Trick upon another. Thus I continued doing great Mischief to the Crown, till my

Officer chancing one Morning to walk Abroad earlier than ordinary, gave me to a Milk-Maid. This Wench bent me, and gave me to her Sweetheart. This ungenerous Gallant marrying her within few Days after, pawned me for a Dram of Brandy, and drinking me out next Day, I was beaten flat with an Hammer, and again set a running.

After many Adventures, which it would be tedious to relate, I was sent to a young Spendthrift, in Company with the Will of his Deceased Father. The young Fellow, who I found was very extravagant, gave great Demonstrations of Joy at the receiving the Will; but opening it, he found himself disinherited and cut off from the Possession of a fair Estate, by Virtue of my being made a Present to him. This put him into such a Passion, that after having taken me in his Hand, and cursed me, he squirred me away from him as far as he could fling me. I chanced to light in an unfrequented Place under a dead Wall, where I lay undiscovered and useless, during the Usurpation of *Oliver Cromwell.*

About a Year after the King's Return, a poor Cavalier that was walking there about Dinner-time fortunately cast his Eye upon me, and, to the great Joy of us both, carried me to a Cook's Shop, where he dined upon me, and drank the King's Health. When I came again into the World, I found that I had been happier in my Retirement than I thought, having probably by that Means escaped wearing a monstrous Pair of Breeches.

Being now of great Credit and Antiquity, I was rather looked upon as a Medal than an ordinary Coin; for which Reason a Gamester laid hold of me, and converted me into a Counter, having got together some Dozens of us for that Use. We led a melancholy Life in his Pos-

session, being busy at those Hours wherein current Coin
is at rest, and partaking the Fate of our Master, being
in a few Moments valued at a Crown, a Pound, or a Six-
pence, according to the Situation in which the Fortune
of the Cards placed us. I had at length the good Luck
to see my Master break, by which Means I was again sent
Abroad under my primitive Denomination of a Shilling.

I shall pass over many other Accidents of less Moment,
and hasten to that fatal Catastrophe when I fell into the
Hands of an Artist who conveyed me under Ground,
and with an unmerciful Pair of Sheers cut off my Titles,
clipped my Brims, retrenched my Shape, rubbed me
to my inmost Ring, and in short, so spoiled and pillaged
me, that he did not leave me worth a Groat. You may
think what a Confusion I was in to see my self thus cur-
tailed and disfigured. I should have been ashamed to
have shewn my Head, had not all my old Acquaintance
been reduced to the same shameful Figure, excepting
some few that were punched thro' the Belly. In the
midst of this general Calamity, when every Body thought
our Misfortune irretrievable, and our Case desperate,
we were thrown into the Furnace together, and (as it
often happens with Cities rising out of a Fire) appeared
with greater Beauty and Lustre than we could ever boast
of before. What has happened to me since this Change
of Sex which you now see, I shall take some other Opportunity to relate. In the mean Time I shall only repeat
two Adventures, as being very extraordinary, and neither
of them having ever happened to me above once in my
Life. The first was, my being in a Poet's Pocket, who
was so taken with the Brightness and Novelty of my
Appearance, that it gave Occasion to the finest Burlesque
Poem in the *British* language, entituled from me, *The*

Splendid Shilling. The second Adventure, which I must not omit, happened to me in the Year 1703, when I was given away in Charity to a blind Man; but indeed this was by Mistake, the Person who gave me having heedlessly thrown me into the Hat among a Pennyworth of Farthings.

A VISION OF MIRZAH

. . . . Omnem, quae non obducta tuenti
Mortales hebetat visus tibi, et humida circum
Caligat, nubem eripiam . . .

Virgil.

When I was at *Grand Cairo* I picked up several Oriental Manuscripts, which I have still by me. Among others I met with one, entituled *The Visions of Mirzah*, which I have read over with great Pleasure. I intend to give it to the Publick when I have no other Entertainment for them; and shall begin with the first Vision, which I have translated Word for Word as follows.

" On the fifth Day of the Moon, which according to the Custom of my Forefathers I always keep holy, after having washed my self and offered up my Morning Devotions, I ascended the high Hills of *Bagdat*, in order to pass the rest of the Day in Meditation and Prayer. As I was here airing my self on the Tops of the Mountains, I fell into a profound Contemplation on the Vanity of humane Life; and passing from one Thought to another, Surely, said I, Man is but a Shadow and Life a Dream. Whilst I was thus musing, I cast my Eyes towards the Summit of a Rock that was not far from me, where I discovered one in the Habit of a Shepherd, with

a little Musical Instrument in his Hand. As I looked
upon him he applied it to his Lips, and began to play
upon it. The Sound of it was exceeding sweet, and
wrought into a Variety of Tunes that were inexpressibly
melodious, and altogether different from any thing I had
ever heard. They put me in mind of those heavenly Airs
that are played to the departed Souls of good Men upon
their first Arrival in Paradise, to wear out the Impressions of the last Agonies, and qualify them for the
Pleasures of that happy Place. My Heart melted away
in secret Raptures.

" I had been often told that the Rock before me was
the Haunt of a Genius; and that several had been enter-
tained with Musick who had passed by it, but never heard
that the Musician had before made himself visible.
When he had raised my Thoughts, by those transporting
Airs which he played, to taste the Pleasures of his Conversation, as I looked upon him like one astonished, he
beckoned to me, and by the waving of his Hand directed
me to approach the Place where he sat. I drew near with
that Reverence which is due to a superior Nature; and
as my Heart was entirely subdued by the captivating
Strains I had heard, I fell down at his Feet and wept.
The Genius smiled upon me with a look of Compassion
and Affability that familiarized him to my Imagination,
and at once dispelled all the Fears and Apprehensions
with which I approached him. He lifted me from the
Ground, and taking me by the Hand, *Mirzah*, said he,
I have heard thee in thy Soliloquies, follow me.

" He then led me to the highest Pinnacle of the Rock,
and placing me on the Top of it, Cast thy Eyes Eastward,
said he, and tell me what thou seest. I see, said I, a
huge Valley, and a prodigious Tide of Water rolling

through it. The Valley that thou seest, said he, is the Vale of Misery, and the Tide of Water that thou seest is Part of the great Tide of Eternity. What is the Reason, said I, that the Tide I see rises out of a thick Mist at one End, and again loses it self in a thick Mist at the other? What thou seest, said he, is that Portion of Eternity which is called Time, measured out by the Sun, and reaching from the Beginning of the World to its Consummation. Examine now, said he, this Sea that is bounded with Darkness at both Ends, and tell me what thou discoverest in it. I see a Bridge, said I, standing in the Midst of the Tide. The Bridge thou seest, said he, is humane Life; consider it attentively. Upon a more leisurely Survey of it, I found that it consisted of threescore and ten entire Arches, with several broken Arches, which added to those that were entire, made up the Number about an hundred. As I was counting the Arches, the Genius told me that this Bridge consisted at first of a thousand Arches; but that a great Flood swept away the rest, and left the Bridge in the ruinous Condition I now beheld it. But tell me further, said he, what thou discoverest on it. I see Multitudes of People passing over it, said I, and a black Cloud hanging on each End of it. As I looked more attentively, I saw several of the Passengers dropping thro' the Bridge, into the great Tide that flowed underneath it; and upon further Examination, perceived there were innumerable Trap-doors that lay concealed in the Bridge, which the Passengers no sooner trod upon, but they fell through them into the Tide and immediately disappeared. These hidden Pit-falls were set very thick at the Entrance of the Bridge, so that throngs of People no sooner broke through the Cloud, but many of them fell into them.

They grew thinner towards the Middle, but multiplied and lay closer together towards the End of the Arches that were entire.

" There were indeed some Persons, but their Number was very small, that continued a kind of hobbling March on the broken Arches, but fell through one after another, being quite tired and spent with so long a Walk.

" I passed some Time in the Contemplation of this wonderful Structure, and the great Variety of Objects which it presented. My Heart was filled with a deep Melancholy to see several dropping unexpectedly in the Midst of Mirth and Jollity, and catching at every thing that stood by to save themselves. Some were looking up towards the Heavens in a thoughtful Posture, and in the Midst of a Speculation stumbled and fell out of Sight. Multitudes were very busy in the Pursuit of Bubbles that glittered in their Eyes and danced before them, but often when they thought themselves within the Reach of them their Footing failed and down they sunk. In this Confusion of Objects, I observed some with Scymetars in their Hands, who ran to and fro upon the Bridge, thrusting several Persons on Trap-doors which did not seem to lie in their Way, and which they might have escaped had they not been thus forced upon them.

" The Genius seeing me indulge my self in this melancholy Prospect, told me I had dwelt long enough upon it: Take thine Eyes off the Bridge, said he, and tell me if thou yet seest any thing thou dost not comprehend. Upon looking up, What mean, said I, those great Flights of Birds that are perpetually hovering about the Bridge, and settling upon it from Time to Time? I see Vultures, Harpyes, Ravens, Cormorants; and among many other feathered Creatures several little winged Boys, that perch in great Numbers upon the middle Arches. These, said the Genius, are Envy, Avarice, Superstition, Despair, Love, with the like Cares and Passions that infest humane Life.

" I here fetched a deep Sigh, Alas, said I, Man was made in vain! How is he given away to Misery and Mortality! tortured in Life, and swallowed up in Death! The Genius being moved with Compassion towards me, bid me quit so uncomfortable a Prospect: Look no more, said he, on Man in the first Stage of his Existence, in his setting out for Eternity; but cast thine Eye on that thick Mist into which the Tide bears the several Generations of Mortals that fall into it. I directed my Sight as I was ordered, and (whether or no the good Genius strengthened it with any supernatural Force, or dissipated Part of the Mist that was before too thick for the Eye to penetrate) I saw the Valley opening at the further End, and spreading forth into an immense Ocean, that had a huge Rock of Adamant running through the Midst of it, and dividing it into two equal Parts. The Clouds still rested on one Half of it, insomuch that I could discover nothing in it; but the other appeared to me a vast Ocean planted with innumerable Islands, that were covered with Fruits and Flowers, and interwoven with a thousand little shining Seas that ran among them. I could see Persons dressed in glorious Habits, with Garlands upon their Heads, passing among the Trees, lying down by the Sides of Fountains, or resting on Beds of Flowers; and could hear a confused Harmony of singing Birds, falling Waters, humane Voices, and musical Instruments. Gladness grew in me upon the Discovery of so delightful a Scene. I wished for the Wings of an Eagle, that I might fly away to those happy Seats; but the Genius told me there was no Passage to them, except through the Gates of Death that I saw opening every Moment upon the Bridge. The Islands, said he, that lie so fresh and green before thee, and with which the whole Face of the Ocean appears spotted as far as thou canst see, are more in Number than the Sands on the Sea-shore; there are Myriads of Islands behind those which thou here discoverest, reaching further than thine Eye or even thine Imagination can extend it self. These are the Mansions of good Men after Death, who according to the Degree and Kinds of Virtue in which they excelled, are distributed among these several Islands, which abound with Pleasures of different Kinds and Degrees, suitable to the Relishes and Perfections of those who are settled in them; every Island is a Paradise accommodated to its respective inhabitants. Are not these, O *Mirzah*, Habitations worth contending for? Does Life appear miserable, that gives thee Opportunities of earning such a Reward? Is Death to be feared, that will convey thee to so happy an Existence? Think not Man was made in vain, who has such an Eternity reserved for him. I gazed with inexpressible pleasure on these happy Islands. At length, said I, shew me now, I beseech thee, the Secrets that lie hid under those dark Clouds which cover the Ocean on the other Side of the Rock of Adamant. The Genius making me no Answer, I turned about to address my self to him a second time, but I found that he had left me; I then turned again to the Vision which I had been so long contemplating, but instead of the rolling Tide, the arched Bridge, and the happy Islands, I saw nothing but the long hollow Valley of *Bagdat*, with Oxen, Sheep, and Camels grazing upon the Sides of it."

ALEXANDER POPE

(1688–1744)

Alexander Pope was born in London in 1688. His father was a well-to-do linen draper and a Roman Catholic, and Pope remained faithful to that religion. He was a very precocious child, writing quite creditable poetry at a very early age (he is said to have written " Happy the man whose wish and care " at the age of nine), and became widely known as a poet in his own day. Deformed and ill-natured, he looked askance on the rest of the world, and it is for his savage satires that he is chiefly remembered. He wrote comparatively little prose. The essay which follows is a good example of his satire, though a very mild one.

ON EPIC POETRY

Docebo
Unde parentur opes; quid alat formetque poetam
Hor. *Ars Poet.* 306.

It is no small pleasure to me, who am zealous in the interests of learning, to think I may have the honour of leading the town into a very new and uncommon road of criticism. As that kind of literature is at present carried on, it consists only in a knowledge of mechanic rules which contribute to the structure of different sorts of poetry; as the receipts of good housewives do to the making puddings of flour, oranges, plums, or any other ingredients. It would, methinks, make these my instructions more easily intelligible to ordinary readers,

if I discoursed of these matters in the style in which
ladies learned in economies dictate to their pupils for the
improvement of the kitchen and larder.

I shall begin with epic poetry, because the critics
agree it is the greatest work human nature is capable
of. I know the French have already laid down many
mechanical rules for compositions of this sort, but at
the same time they cut off almost all undertakers from
the possibility of ever performing them; for the first
qualification they unanimously require in a poet, is a
genius. I shall here endeavour (for the benefit of my
countrymen) to make it manifest, that epic poems may
be made " without a genius ", nay, without learning or
much reading. This must necessarily be of great use to
all those poets who confess they never read, and of whom
the world is convinced they never learn. What Molière
observes of making a dinner, that any man can do it with
money, and if a professed cook cannot without, he has
his art for nothing; the same may be said of making a
poem, it is easily brought about by him that has a genius,
but the skill lies in doing it without one. In pursuance
of this end, I shall present the reader with a plain and
certain receipt, by which even sonneteers and ladies may
be qualified for this grand performance.

I know it will be objected that one of the chief qualifications of an epic poet is to be knowing in all arts and
sciences. But this ought not to discourage those that
have no learning, as long as indexes and dictionaries may
be had, which are the compendium of all knowledge.
Besides, since it is an established rule that none of the
terms of those arts and sciences are to be made use of,
one may venture to affirm, our poet cannot impertinently
offend in this point. The learning which will be more

particularly necessary to him, is the ancient geography of towns, mountains, and rivers: for this let him take Cluverius, value fourpence.

Another quality required is a complete skill in languages. To this I answer, that it is notorious persons of no genius have been oftentimes great linguists. To instance in the Greek, of which there are two sorts: the original Greek, and that from which our modern authors translate. I should be unwilling to promise impossibilities, but modestly speaking, this may be learned in about an hour's time with ease. I have known one, who became a sudden professor of Greek immediately upon application of the left-hand page of the Cambridge Homer to his eye. It is in these days with authors as with other men, the well-bred are familiarly acquainted with them at first sight; and as it is sufficient for a good general to have surveyed the ground he is to conquer, so it is enough for a good poet to have seen the author he is to be master of. But to proceed to the purpose of this paper.

A RECEIPT TO MAKE AN EPIC POEM

FOR THE FABLE

Take out of any old poem, history book, romance, or legend (for instance, Geoffrey of Monmouth, or Don Belianis of Greece), those parts of story which afford most scope for long descriptions. Put these pieces together, and throw all the adventures you fancy into one tale. Then take a hero whom you may choose for the sound of his name, and put him into the midst of these adventures. There let him work for twelve books; at the end of which you may take him out ready prepared to conquer, or to marry; it being necessary that the conclusion of an epic poem be fortunate.

To make an Episode. — Take any remaining adventure of your former collection, in which you could no way involve your hero; or any unfortunate accident that was too good to be thrown away; and it will be of use applied to any other person, who may be lost and evaporate in the course of the work, without the least damage to the composition.

For the Moral and Allegory. — These you may extract out of the fable afterwards, at your leisure. Be sure you strain them sufficiently.

FOR THE MANNERS

For those of the hero, take all the best qualities you can find in all the celebrated heroes of antiquity; if they will not be reduced to a consistency, lay them all on a heap upon him. But be sure they are qualities which your patron would be thought to have; and, to prevent any mistake which the world may be subject to, select from the alphabet those capital letters that compose his name, and set them at the head of a dedication before your poem. However, do not absolutely observe the exact quantity of these virtues, it not being determined whether or no it be necessary for the hero of the poem to be an honest man. For the under characters, gather them from Homer and Virgil, and change the names as occasion serves.

FOR THE MACHINES

Take of deities, male and female, as many as you can use. Separate them into two equal parts, and keep Jupiter in the middle. Let Juno put him in a ferment, and Venus mollify him. Remember on all occasions to make use of volatile Mercury. If you have need of devils, draw them out of Milton's Paradise, and extract your spirits from Tasso. The use of these machines is evident; and since no epic poem can possibly subsist without them, the wisest way is to reserve them for your greatest necessities. When you cannot extricate your hero by any human means, or yourself by your own wits, seek relief from heaven, and the gods will do your business very readily. This is according to the direct prescription of Horace in his *Art of Poetry*:

> *Nec deus intersit, nisi dignus vindice nodus*
> *Inciderit.*

> Never presume to make a God appear,
> But for a business worthy of a God.—ROSCOMMON.

That is to say, a poet should never call upon the gods for their assistance but when he is in great perplexity.

FOR THE DESCRIPTIONS

For a Tempest. — Take Eurus, Zephyr, Auster, and Boreas, and cast them together in one verse. Add to these of rain, lightning, and of thunder (the loudest you can) *quantum sufficit*. Mix your clouds and billows well together until they foam, and thicken your description here and there with a quicksand. Brew your tempest well in your head, before you set a-blowing.

For a Battle. — Pick a large quantity of images and descriptions from Homer's *Iliad*, with a spice or two of Virgil, and if there remain any overplus you may lay them by for a skirmish. Season it well with similes, and it will make an excellent battle.

For Burning a Town. — If such a description be necessary, because it is certain there is one in Virgil, Old Troy is ready burnt to your hands. But if you fear that would be thought borrowed, a chapter or two of the *Theory of the Conflagration*, well circumstanced, and done into verse, will be a good succedaneum.

As for *Similes and Metaphors*, they may be found all over the creation; the most ignorant may gather them, but the danger is in applying them. For this, advise with your bookseller.

FOR THE LANGUAGE

(I mean the diction.) Here it will do well to be an imitator of Milton, for you will find it easier to imitate him in this than anything else. Hebraisms and Grecisms are to be found in him, without the trouble of learning the languages. I knew a painter, who (like our poet) had no genius, made his daubings to be thought originals by setting them in the smoke. You may in the same manner give the venerable air of antiquity to your piece, by darkening it up and down with Old English. With this you may be easily furnished upon any occasion by the dictionary commonly printed at the end of Chaucer.

I must not conclude, without cautioning all writers without genius in one material point, which is, never to be afraid of having too much fire in their works. I should advise rather to take their warmest thoughts, and spread them abroad upon paper; for they are observed to cool before they are read.

OLIVER GOLDSMITH

(1728–1774)

Oliver Goldsmith, the son of a poor Irish parson, and one of the most lovable of scamps, was born in Ireland in 1728. After a harum-scarum boyhood, he spent his time as a student getting into scrapes; then, after a happy-go-lucky tour on the Continent, he arrived almost penniless in London. After vainly trying his hand at various kinds of work, he turned at last to literature. As well as essays, he wrote excellent verse, two very successful comedies, and one novel, *The Vicar of Wakefield*, which was based on his own boyhood. He was ugly, vain, and foolish, extremely ignorant, quite unpractical, and absurdly generous; but his innate charm redeemed his faults, and his essays are among the greatest in English literature. The three which follow are probably the best known. Although he was well paid for most of his work, he died in his normal state of poverty in 1774.

THE MAN IN BLACK

Though fond of many acquaintances, I desire an intimacy only with a few. The Man in Black, whom I have often mentioned, is one whose friendship I could wish to acquire, because he possesses my esteem. His manners, it is true, are tinctured with some strange inconsistencies; and he may be justly termed an humorist in a nation of humorists. Though he is generous even to profusion, he affects to be thought a prodigy of parsimony and prudence; though his conversation be replete with the most sordid and selfish maxims, his heart is dilated with the most unbounded love. I have known him profess himself a man-hater, while his cheek was glowing with compassion; and, while his looks were softened into pity, I have heard him use the language of the most unbounded ill-nature. Some affect humanity and tenderness, others boast of having such dispositions from Nature; but he is the only man I ever knew who seemed ashamed of his natural benevolence. He takes as much pains to hide his feelings, as any hypocrite would to conceal his indifference; but on every unguarded moment the mask drops off, and reveals him to the most superficial observer.

In one of our late excursions into the country, happening to discourse upon the provision that was made for the poor in England, he seemed amazed how any of his countrymen could be so foolishly weak as to relieve occasional objects of charity, when the laws had made such ample provision for their support. "In every parish-house," says he, "the poor are supplied with food, clothes, fire, and a bed to lie on; they want no more, I desire no more myself; yet still they seem discontented. I'm surprised at the inactivity of our magistrates in not taking up such vagrants, who are only a weight upon the industrious; I'm surprised that the people are found to relieve them, when they must be at the same time sensible that it, in some measure, encourages idleness, extravagance, and imposture. Were I to advise any man for whom I had the least regard, I would caution him by all means not to be imposed upon by their false pretences: let me assure you, sir, they are impostors, every one of them; and rather merit a prison than relief."

He was proceeding in this strain earnestly, to dissuade me from an imprudence of which I am seldom guilty, when an old man, who still had about him the remnants of tattered finery, implored our compassion. He assured us that he was no common beggar, but forced into the shameful profession to support a dying wife and five hungry children. Being prepossessed against such falsehoods, his story had not the least influence upon me; but it was quite otherwise with the Man in Black; I could see it visibly operate upon his countenance, and effectually interrupt his harangue. I could easily perceive that his heart burned to relieve the five starving children, but he seemed ashamed to discover his weakness to me. While he thus hesitated between compassion and pride, I pretended to look another way, and he seized this opportunity of giving the poor petitioner a piece of silver, bidding him at the same time, in order that I should hear, go work for his bread, and not tease passengers with such impertinent falsehoods for the future.

As he had fancied himself quite unperceived, he continued, as we proceeded, to rail against beggars with as much animosity as before; he threw in some episodes on his own amazing prudence and economy, with his profound skill in discovering impostors; he explained the manner in which he would deal with beggars, were he a magistrate, hinted at enlarging some of the prisons for their reception, and told two stories of ladies that were robbed by beggarmen. He was beginning a third to the same purpose, when a sailor with a wooden leg once more crossed our walks, desiring our pity, and blessing our limbs. I was for going on without taking any notice, but my friend, looking wistfully upon the poor petitioner, bade me stop, and he would show me with how much ease he could at any time detect an impostor.

He now, therefore, assumed a look of importance, and in an angry tone began to examine the sailor, demanding in what engagement he was thus disabled and rendered unfit for service. The sailor replied in a tone as angrily as he, that he had been an officer on board a private ship of war, and that he had lost his leg abroad, in defence of those who did nothing at home. At this reply, all my friend's importance vanished in a moment; he had not a single question more to ask; he now only studied what method he should take to relieve him unobserved. He had, however, no easy part to act, as he was obliged to preserve the appearance of ill-nature before me, and yet relieve himself by relieving the sailor. Casting, therefore, a furious look upon some bundles of chips which the fellow carried in a string at his back, my friend demanded how he sold his matches; but not waiting for a reply, desired in a surly tone to have a shilling's worth. The sailor seemed at first surprised at his demand, but soon recollecting himself, and presenting his whole bundle — " Here, master," says he, " take all my cargo, and a blessing into the bargain."

It is impossible to describe with what an air of triumph my friend marched off with his new purchase; he assured me that he was firmly of opinion that those fellows must have stolen their goods who could thus afford to sell them for half value. He informed me of several different uses to which those chips might be applied; he expatiated largely upon the savings that would result from lighting candles with a match instead of thrusting them into the fire. He averred that he would as soon have parted with a tooth as his money to those vagabonds, unless for some valuable consideration. I cannot tell how long this panegyric upon frugality and matches might have continued, had not his attention been called off by another object more distressful than either of the former. A woman in rags, with one child in her arms, and another on her back, was attempting to sing ballads, but with such a mournful voice that it was difficult to determine whether she was singing or crying. A wretch who in the deepest distress still aimed at good-humour, was an object my friend was by no means capable of withstanding; his vivacity and his discourse were instantly interrupted; upon this occasion his very dissimulation had forsaken him. Even in my presence, he immediately applied his hands to his pockets, in order to relieve her; but guess his confusion, when he found he had already given away all the money he carried about him to former objects. The misery painted in the woman's visage was not half so strongly expressed as the agony in his. He continued to search for some time, but to no purpose, till, at length, recollecting himself, with a face of ineffable good-nature, as he had no money, he put into her hands his shilling's worth of matches.

BEAU TIBBS

Though naturally pensive, yet I am fond of gay company, and take every opportunity of thus dismissing the mind from duty. From this motive I am often found in the centre of a crowd; and wherever pleasure is to be sold, am always a purchaser. In those places, without being remarked by any, I join in whatever goes forward; work my passions into a similitude of frivolous earnestness, shout as they shout, and condemn as they happen to disapprove. A mind thus sunk for awhile below its natural standard, is qualified for stronger flights, as those first retire who would spring forward with greater vigour.

Attracted by the serenity of the evening, a friend and I lately went to gaze upon the company in one of the public walks near the city. Here we sauntered together for some time, either praising the beauty of such as were handsome, or the dresses of such as had nothing else to recommend them. We had gone thus deliberately forward for some time, when my friend, stopping on a sudden, caught me by the elbow, and led me out of the public walk. I could perceive by the quickness of his pace, and by his frequently looking behind, that he was attempting to avoid somebody who followed; we now turned to the right, then to the left; as we went forward, he still went faster, but in vain; the person whom he attempted to escape, hunted us through every doubling, and gained upon us each moment; so that at last we fairly stood still, resolving to face what we could not avoid.

Our pursuer soon came up, and joined us with all the familiarity of an old acquaintance. " My dear Charles," cries he, shaking my friend's hand, " where have you been hiding this half a century? Positively I had fancied you were gone down to cultivate matrimony and your estate in the country." During the reply I had an opportunity of surveying the appearance of our new companion. His hat was pinched up with peculiar smartness; his looks were pale, thin, and sharp; round his neck he wore a broad black ribbon, and in his bosom a buckle studded with glass; his coat was trimmed with tarnished twist; he wore by his side a sword with a black hilt, and his stockings of silk, though newly washed, were grown yellow by long service. I was so much engaged with the peculiarity of his dress, that I attended only to the latter part of my friend's reply, in which he complimented Mr. Tibbs on the taste of his clothes, and the bloom in his

countenance. " Psha, psha, Charles," cried the figure,
" no more of that if you love me; you know I hate flattery,
on my soul I do; and yet, to be sure, an intimacy with
the great will improve one's appearance, and a course of
venison will fatten; and yet, faith, I despise the great
as much as you do; but there are a great many honest
fellows among them; and we must not quarrel with one
half because the other wants breeding. If they were all
such as my Lord Mudler, one of the most good-natured
creatures that ever squeezed a lemon, I should myself
be among the number of their admirers. I was yesterday
to dine at the Duchess of Piccadilly's. My lord was
there. ' Ned,' says he to me, ' Ned,' says he, ' I'll
hold gold to silver I can tell where you were poaching
last night.' ' Poaching, my lord?' says I; ' faith, you
have missed already; for I stayed at home, and let
the girls poach for me. That's my way; I take a fine
woman as some animals do their prey; stand still, and
swoop, they fall into my mouth.' "

" Ah, Tibbs, thou art an happy fellow," cried my
companion, with looks of infinite pity; " I hope your
fortune is as much improved as your understanding in
such company?" " Improved," replied the other; " you
shall know — but let it go no further — a great secret
— five hundred a year to begin with. My lord's word
of honour for it. His lordship took me down in his own
chariot yesterday, and we had a *tête-à-tête* dinner in the
country; where we talked of nothing else." " I fancy
you forgot, sir," cried I; " you told us but this moment
of your dining yesterday in town." " Did I say so?"
replied he coolly. " To be sure, if I said so it was so.
Dined in town: egad, now I do remember, I did dine
in town; but I dined in the country too; for you must

know, my boys, I eat two dinners. By the bye, I am grown as nice as the devil in my eating. I'll tell you a pleasant affair about that: We were a select party of us to dine at Lady Grogram's, an affected piece, but let it go no further; a secret. 'Well,' says I, 'I'll hold a thousand guineas, and say done first, that——' But, dear Charles, you are an honest creature, lend me half-a-crown for a minute or two, or so, just till —— But, harkee, ask me for it the next time we meet, or it may be twenty to one but I forget to pay you."

When he left us, our conversation naturally turned upon so extraordinary a character. "His very dress," cries my friend, "is not less extraordinary than his conduct. If you meet him this day you find him in rags; if the next, in embroidery. With those persons of distinction, of whom he talks so familiarly, he has scarce a coffee-house acquaintance. However, both for the interests of society, and perhaps for his own, Heaven has made him poor; and while all the world perceives his wants, he fancies them concealed from every eye. An agreeable companion, because he understands flattery; and all must be pleased with the first part of his conversation, though all are sure of its ending with a demand on their purse. While his youth countenances the levity of his conduct, he may thus earn a precarious subsistence; but when age comes on, the gravity of which is incompatible with buffoonery, then will he find himself forsaken by all; condemned, in the decline of life, to hang upon some rich family whom he once despised, there to undergo all the ingenuity of studied contempt, to be employed only as a spy upon the servants, or a bug-bear to fright children into duty."

BEAU TIBBS AT HOME

There are some acquaintances whom it is no easy matter to shake off. My little beau yesterday overtook me again in one of the public walks, and, slapping me on the shoulder, saluted me with an air of the most perfect familiarity. His dress was the same as usual, except that he had more powder in his hair; wore a dirtier shirt, and had on a pair of temple spectacles, and his hat under his arm.

As I knew him to be an harmless amusing little thing, I could not return his smiles with any degree of severity; so we walked forward on the terms of the utmost intimacy, and in a few minutes discussed all the usual topics preliminary to particular conversation.

The oddities that marked his character, however, soon began to appear; he bowed to several well-dressed persons, who, by their manner of returning the compliment, appeared perfect strangers. At intervals he drew out a pocket-book, seeming to take memorandums before all the company, with much importance and assiduity. In this manner he led me through the length of the whole Mall, fretting at his absurdities, and fancying myself laughed at as well as he by every spectator.

When we were got to the end of our procession, " Hang me," cries he, with an air of vivacity, " I never saw the park so thin in my life before; there's no company at all to-day. Not a single face to be seen." " No company," interrupted I, peevishly; " no company where there is such a crowd? Why, man, there is too much. What are the thousands that have been laughing at us but company?" " Lord, my dear," returned he, with the utmost good humour, " you seem immensely chagrined; but, hang me, when the world laughs at me, I laugh at all the world, and so we are even. My Lord Trip, Bill Squash, the Creolian, and I, sometimes make a party at being ridiculous; and so we say and do a thousand things for the joke's sake. But I see you are grave; and if you are for a fine grave sentimental companion, you shall dine with my wife to-day; I must insist on 't; I'll introduce you to Mrs. Tibbs, a lady of as elegant qualifications as any in nature; she was bred, but that's between ourselves, under the inspection of the Countess of Shoreditch. A charming body of voice! But no more of that, she shall give us a song. You shall see my little girl too. Carolina Wilhelma Amelia Tibbs, a sweet pretty creature; I design her for my Lord Drumstick's eldest son; but that's in friendship, let it go no further; she's but six years old, and yet she walks a minuet, and plays on the guitar immensely already. I intend she shall be as perfect as possible in every accomplishment. In the first place I'll make her a scholar; I'll teach her Greek myself, and I intend to learn that language purposely to instruct her; but let that be a secret."

Thus saying, without waiting for a reply, he took me by the arm and hauled me along. We passed through many dark alleys and winding ways; for, from some motives to me unknown, he seemed to have a particular aversion to every frequented street; at last, however, we got to the door of a dismal-looking house in the outlets of the town, where he informed me he chose to reside for the benefit of the air.

We entered the lower door, which seemed ever to lie most hospitably open: and I began to ascend an old and creaking staircase, when, as he mounted to show me the way, he demanded whether I delighted in prospects; to which answering in the affirmative, " Then," says he, " I shall show you one of the most charming out of my windows; we shall see the ships sailing, and the whole country for twenty miles round, tip top, quite high. My Lord Swamp would give ten thousand guineas for such a one; but, as I sometimes pleasantly tell him, I always love to keep my prospects at home, that my friends may come to see me the oftener."

By this time we were arrived as high as the stairs would permit us to ascend, till we came to what he was facetiously pleased to call the first floor down the chimney; and knocking at the door, a voice, with a Scotch accent, from within, demanded, " Wha's there?" My conductor answered that it was him. But this not satisfying the querist, the voice again repeated the demand: to which he answered louder than before, and now the door was opened by an old maid-servant with cautious reluctance.

When we were got in, he welcomed me to his house with great ceremony, and turning to the old woman, asked where her lady was? " Good troth," replied she, in the northern dialect, " she's washing your twa shirts at the next door, because they have taken an oath against lending out the tub any longer." " My two shirts!" cries he in a tone that faltered with confusion, " what does the idiot mean?" " I ken what I mean well enough," replied the other; " she's washing your twa shirts at the next door, because ——" " Fire and fury! no more of thy stupid explanations," cried he. " Go and inform her we have got company. Were that Scotch hag," continued he, turning to me, " to be for ever in the family, she would never learn politeness, nor forget that absurd poisonous accent of hers, or testify the smallest specimen of breeding or high life; and yet it is very surprising too, as I had her from a parliament man, a friend of mine, from the Highlands, one of the politest men in the world; but that's a secret."

We waited some time for Mrs. Tibbs' arrival, during which interval I had a full opportunity of surveying the chamber and all its furniture; which consisted of four chairs with old wrought bottoms, that he assured me were his wife's embroidery; a square table that had been once japanned, a cradle in one corner, a lumbering cabinet in the other; a broken shepherdess, and a mandarin without a head, were stuck over the chimney; and round the walls several paltry, unframed pictures, which, he observed, were all of his own drawing. " What do you think, sir, of that head in the corner, done in the manner of Grisoni? There's the true keeping in it; it's my own face: and though there happens to be no likeness, a countess offered me an hundred for its fellow: I refused her; for, hang it, that would be mechanical, you know."

The wife, at last, made her appearance, at once a slattern and a coquette; much emaciated, but still carrying the remains of beauty. She made twenty apologies for being seen in such odious dishabille, but hoped to be excused, as she had stayed out all night at Vauxhall Gardens with the countess, who was excessively fond of the horns. " And indeed, my dear," added she, turning to her husband, " his lordship drank your health in a bumper." " Poor Jack," cries he, " a dear good-natured creature, I know he loves me; but I hope, my dear, you have given orders for dinner? You need make no great preparations neither, there are but three of us; something elegant, and little will do; a turbot, an ortolan, or a ——"

" Or what do you think, my dear," interrupts the wife,
" of a nice pretty bit of ox-cheek, piping hot, and dressed
with a little of my own sauce?" " The very thing,"
replies he; " it will eat best with some smart bottled
beer; but be sure to let's have the sauce his grace was so
fond of. I hate your immense loads of meat; that is
country all over; extreme disgusting to those who are
in the least acquainted with high life."

By this time my curiosity began to abate, and my
appetite to increase; the company of fools may at first
make us smile, but at last never fails of rendering us
melancholy. I therefore pretended to recollect a prior
engagement, and after having shown my respect to the
house, by giving the old servant a piece of money at
the door, I took my leave: Mr. Tibbs assuring me that
dinner, if I stayed, would be ready at least in less than
two hours.

CHARLES LAMB

(1775–1834)

Charles Lamb, almost better known as Elia, was the gentlest and most kindly of men. Born in London in 1775, the son of a lawyer's clerk, he was well if humbly educated, and spent an unexciting life as a clerk in the South Sea House. His private life was a sad one; he devoted himself to looking after his sister Mary, who was subject to fits of insanity, in one of which she stabbed her mother to death (Mary is the Barbara of many of the essays; something of the gentle pathos of their life will be found in the essay on Dream Children). As well as essays Lamb wrote a little verse, in the same gently pathetic strain; and he and his sister, who had also real literary ability, collaborated in tales from Shakespeare retold for children. It is impossible to represent Lamb adequately in a brief anthology; the four essays which follow have been chosen to illustrate his ability in humour and pathos, and his pleasant narrative style.

MRS. BATTLE'S OPINIONS ON WHIST

" A clear fire, a clean hearth, and the rigour of the game." This was the celebrated *wish* of old Sarah Battle (now with God) who, next to her devotions, loved a good game at whist. She was none of your lukewarm gamesters, your half and half players, who have no objection to take a hand if you want one to make up a rubber; who affirm that they have no pleasure in winning; that they like to win one game and lose another; that they can while away an hour very agreeably at a card-table, but are indifferent whether they play or no; and will desire an adversary, who has slipt a wrong card, to take it up and play another. These insufferable triflers are the curse of a table. One of these flies will spoil a whole pot. Of such it may be said, that they do not play at cards, but only play at playing at them.

Sarah Battle was none of that breed. She detested them, as I do, from her heart and soul; and would not, save upon a striking emergency, willingly seat herself at the same table with them. She loved a thorough-paced partner, a determined enemy. She took, and gave, no concessions. She hated favours. She never made a revoke, nor ever passed it over in her adversary without exacting the utmost forfeiture. She fought a good fight: cut and thrust. She held not her good sword (her cards) " like a dancer ". She sat bolt upright; and neither showed you her cards, nor desired to see yours. All people have their blind side — their superstitions; and I have heard her declare, under the rose, that Hearts was her favourite suit.

I never in my life — and I knew Sarah Battle many of the best years of it — saw her take out her snuff-box when it was her turn to play; or snuff a candle in the middle of a game; or ring for a servant, till it was fairly over. She never introduced or connived at, miscellaneous conversations during its process. As she emphatically observed, cards were cards: and if I ever saw unmingled distaste in her fine last-century countenance, it was at the airs of a young gentleman of a literary turn, who had been with difficulty persuaded to take a hand; and who, in his excess of candour, declared, that he thought there was no harm in unbending the mind now and then, after serious studies, in recreations of that kind! She could not bear to have her noble occupation, to which she wound up her faculties, considered in that light. It was her business, her duty, the thing she came into the world to do, — and she did it. She unbent her mind afterwards — over a book.

Pope was her favourite author: his Rape of the Lock her favourite work. She once did me the favour to play over with me (with the cards) his celebrated game of Ombre in that poem; and to explain to me how far it agreed with, and in what points it would be found to differ from, tradrille. Her illustrations were apposite and poignant; and I had the pleasure of sending the substance of them to Mr. Bowles: but I suppose they came too late to be inserted among his ingenious notes upon that author.

Quadrille, she has often told me, was her first love; but whist had engaged her maturer esteem. The former, she said, was showy and specious, and likely to allure young persons. The uncertainty and quick shifting of partners — a thing which the constancy of whist abhors; the dazzling supremacy and regal investiture of Spadille — absurd, as she justly observed, in the pure aristocracy of whist, where his crown and garter gave him no proper power above his brother-nobility of the Aces; — the giddy vanity, so taking to the inexperienced, of playing alone; — above all, the overpowering attractions of a *Sans Prendre Vole*, — to the triumph of which there is certainly nothing parallel or approaching, in the contingencies of whist; — all these, she would say, made quadrille a game of captivation to the young and enthusiastic. But whist was the *solider* game: that was her word. It was a long meal; not like quadrille, a feast of snatches. One or two rubbers might co-extend in duration with an evening. They gave time to form rooted friendships, to cultivate steady enmities. She despised the chance-started, capricious, and ever fluctuating alliances of the other. The skirmishes of quadrille, she would say, reminded her of the petty ephemeral embroilments of the little Italian states, depicted by Machiavel; perpetually changing postures and connections; bitter foes to-day, sugared darlings to-morrow; kissing and scratching in a breath; — but the wars of whist were comparable to the long, steady, deep-rooted, rational antipathies of the great French and English nations.

A grave simplicity was what she chiefly admired in her favourite game. There was nothing silly in it, like the nob in cribbage — nothing superfluous. No *flushes* — that most irrational of all pleas that a reasonable being can set up: — that any one should claim four by virtue of holding cards of the same mark and colour, without reference to the playing of the game, or the individual worth or pretensions of the cards themselves! She held this to be a solecism; as pitiful an ambition at cards as alliteration is in authorship. She despised superficiality, and looked deeper than the colours of things. Suits were soldiers, she would say, and must have a uniformity of array to distinguish them: but what should we say to a foolish squire, who should claim a merit for dressing up his tenantry in red jackets, that never were to be marshalled — never to take the field? — She even wished that whist were more simple than it is; and, in my mind, would have stript it of some appendages, which, in the state of human frailty, may be venially, and even commendably allowed of. She saw no reason for the deciding of the trump by the turn of the card. Why not one suit always trumps? — Why two colours, when the mark of the suits would have sufficiently distinguished them without it? —

" But the eye, my dear Madam, is agreeably refreshed with the variety. Man is not a creature of pure reason — he must have his senses delightfully appealed to. We see it in Roman Catholic countries, where the music and the paintings draw in many to worship, whom your quaker spirit of unsensualising would have kept out. — You, yourself, have a pretty collection of paintings — but confess to me, whether, walking in your gallery at Sandham, among those clear Vandykes, or among the Paul Potters in the anteroom, you ever felt your bosom glow with an elegant delight, at all comparable to *that* you have it in your power to experience most evenings over a well-arranged assortment of the court cards? — the pretty antic habits, like heralds in a procession — the gay triumph-assuring scarlets — the contrasting deadly-killing sables — the ' hoary majesty of spades ' — Pam in all his glory! —

" All these might be dispensed with; and, with their naked names upon the drab pasteboard, the game might go on very well, pictureless. But the *beauty* of cards would be extinguished for ever. Stripped of all that is imaginative in them, they must degenerate into mere gambling. Imagine a dull deal board, or drum head, to spread them on, instead of that nice verdant carpet (next to nature's), fittest arena for those courtly combatants to play their gallant jousts and tourneys in! — Exchange those delicately-turned ivory markers — (work of Chinese artist, unconscious of their symbol, — or as profanely slighting their true application as the arrantest Ephesian journeyman that turned out those little shrines for the goddess) — exchange them for little bits of leather (our ancestors' money) or chalk and a slate!" —

The old lady, with a smile, confessed the soundness of my logic; and to her approbation of my arguments on her favourite topic that evening, I have always fancied myself indebted for the legacy of a curious cribbage board, made of the finest Sienna marble, which her maternal uncle (Old Walter Plumer, whom I have elsewhere celebrated) brought with him from Florence: — this, and a trifle of five hundred pounds came to me at her death.

The former bequest (which I do not least value) I have kept with religious care; though she herself, to confess a truth, was never greatly taken with cribbage. It was an essentially vulgar game, I have heard her say, — disputing with her uncle, who was very partial to it. She could never heartily bring her mouth to pronounce " *go* ", or " *that's a go* ". She called it an ungrammatical game. The pegging teased her. I once knew her to forfeit a rubber (a five dollar stake), because she would not take advantage of the turn-up knave, which would have given it her, but which she must have claimed by the disgraceful tenure of declaring " *two for his heels* ". There is something extremely genteel in this sort of self-denial. Sarah Battle was a gentlewoman born.

Piquet she held the best game at the cards for two persons, though she would ridicule the pedantry of the terms — such as pique repique — the capot — they savoured (she thought) of affectation. But games for two, or even three, she never greatly cared for. She loved the quadrate, or square. She would argue thus: — Cards are warfare: the ends are gain, with glory. But cards are war, in disguise of a sport: when single adversaries encounter, the ends proposed are too palpable. By themselves, it is too close a fight: with spectators, it is not much bettered. No looker-on can be interested, except for a bet, and then it is a mere affair of money; he cares not for your luck *sympathetically*, or for your play. — Three are still worse;

a mere naked war of every man against every man, as
in cribbage, without league or alliance; or a rotation
of petty and contradictory interests, a succession of
heartless leagues, and not much more hearty infractions
of them, as in tradrille. But in square games (*she meant
whist*) all that is possible to be attained in card-playing
is accomplished. There are the incentives of profit with
honour, common to every species — though the *latter*
can be but very imperfectly enjoyed in those other
games, where the spectator is only feebly a participator.
But the parties in whist are spectators and principals
too. They are a theatre to themselves, and a looker-on
is not wanted. He is rather worse than nothing, and an
impertinence. Whist abhors neutrality, or interests
beyond its sphere. You glory in some surprising stroke
of skill or fortune, not because a cold — or even an interested — by-stander witnesses it, but because your *partner*
sympathises in the contingency. You win for two. You
triumph for two. Two are exalted. Two again are morti-
fied; which divides their disgrace, as the conjunction
doubles (by taking off the invidiousness) your glories.
Two losing to two are better reconciled, than one to one
in that close butchery. The hostile feeling is weakened
by multiplying the channels. War becomes a civil game.
— By such reasonings as these the old lady was accustomed to defend her favourite pastime.

No inducement could ever prevail upon her to play at
any game where chance entered into the composition,
for nothing. Chance, she would argue — and here again
admire the subtlety of her conclusion! — chance is
nothing, but where something else depends upon it. It is
obvious, that cannot be *glory*. What rational cause of
exultation could it give to a man to turn up size ace a

hundred times together by himself? or before spectators, where no stake is depending? — Make a lottery of
a hundred thousand tickets with but one fortunate
number — and what possible principle of our nature,
except stupid wonderment, could it gratify to gain that
number as many times successively, without a prize? —
Therefore she disliked the mixture of chance in back-
gammon, where it was not played for money. She called
it foolish, and those people idiots, who were taken with
a lucky hit under such circumstances. Games of pure
skill were as little to her fancy. Played for a stake, they
were a mere system of over-reaching. Played for glory,
they were a mere setting of one man's wit — his memory,
or combination-faculty rather — against another's; like a
mock engagement at a review, bloodless and profitless. —
She could not conceive a *game* wanting the spritely in-
fusion of chance, — the handsome excuses of good fortune. Two people playing at chess in a corner of a room
whilst whist was stirring in the centre, would inspire her
with unsufferable horror and ennui. Those well-cut
similitudes of Castles, and Knights, the *imagery* of the
board, she would argue (and I think in this case justly),
were entirely misplaced, and senseless. Those hard head-
contests can in no instance ally with the fancy. They
reject form and colour. A pencil and dry slate (she used
to say) were the proper arena for such combatants.

To those puny objectors against cards, as nurturing
the bad passions, she would retort, that man is a gaming
animal. He must be always trying to get the better in
something or other: — that this passion can scarcely be
more safely expended than upon a game at cards: that
cards are a temporary illusion; in truth, a mere drama;
for we do but *play* at being mightily concerned, where a

few idle shillings are at stake, yet, during the illusion, we *are* as mightily concerned as those whose stake is crowns and kingdoms. They are a sort of dream-fighting; much ado; great battling, and little blood shed; mighty means for disproportioned ends; quite as diverting, and a great deal more innoxious, than many of those more serious *games* of life, which men play, without esteeming them to be such. ——

With great deference to the old lady's judgment on these matters, I think I have experienced some moments in my life, when playing at cards *for nothing* has even been very agreeable. When I am in sickness, or not in the best spirits, I sometimes call for the cards, and play a game at piquet *for love* with my cousin Bridget — Bridget Elia.

I grant there is something sneaking in it: but with a toothache or a sprained ankle, — when you are subdued and humble, — you are glad to pay up with an inferior spring of action.

There is such a thing in nature, I am convinced, as *sick whist.* —

I grant it is not the highest style of man — I deprecate the manes of Sarah Battle — she lives not, alas! to whom I should apologise. —

At such times those *terms* which my old friend objected to, come in as something admissible. — I love to get a tierce or a quatorze, though they mean nothing. I am subdued to an inferior interest. Those shadows of winning amuse me.

That last game I had with my sweet cousin (I capotted her) — (dare I tell thee how foolish I am?) — I wished it might have lasted for ever, though we gained nothing, and lost nothing, though it was a mere shade of play:

I would be content to go on in that idle folly for ever.
The pipkin should be ever boiling, that was to prepare
the gentle lenitive to my foot, which Bridget was doomed
to apply after the game was over: and as I do not much
relish appliances, there it should ever bubble. Bridget
and I should be ever playing.

A DISSERTATION UPON ROAST PIG

Mankind, says a Chinese manuscript, which my friend
M. was obliging enough to read and explain to me, for
the first seventy thousand ages ate their meat raw,
clawing or biting it from the living animal, just as they
do in Abyssinia to this day. This period is not obscurely
hinted at by their great Confucius in the second chapter
of his Mundane Mutations, where he designates a kind
of golden age by the term Cho-fang, literally the Cook's
holiday. The manuscript goes on to say, that the art
of roasting, or rather broiling (which I take to be the
elder brother), was accidentally discovered in the manner
following. The swine-herd, Ho-ti, having gone out into
the woods one morning, as his manner was, to collect
mast for his hogs, left his cottage in the care of his eldest
son Bo-bo, a great lubberly boy, who being fond of playing
with fire, as younkers of his age commonly are, let some
sparks escape into a bundle of straw, which, kindling
quickly, spread the conflagration over every part of their
poor mansion, till it was reduced to ashes. Together
with the cottage (a sorry antediluvian make-shift of a
building, you may think it), what was of much more
importance, a fine litter of new-farrowed pigs, no less
than nine in number, perished. China pigs have been

esteemed a luxury all over the East from the remotest periods that we read of. Bo-bo was in utmost consternation, as you may think, not so much for the sake of the tenement, which his father and he could easily build up again with a few dry branches, and the labour of an hour or two, at any time, as for the loss of the pigs. While he was thinking what he should say to his father, and wringing his hands over the smoking remnants of one of those untimely sufferers, an odour assailed his nostrils, unlike any scent which he had before experienced. What could it proceed from? — not from the burnt cottage — he had smelt that smell before — indeed this was by no means the first accident of the kind which had occurred through the negligence of this unlucky young fire-brand. Much less did it resemble that of any known herb, weed, or flower. A premonitory moistening at the same time overflowed his nether lip. He knew not what to think. He next stooped down to feel the pig, if there were any signs of life in it. He burnt his fingers, and to cool them he applied them in his booby fashion to his mouth. Some of the crums of the scorched skin had come away with his fingers, and for the first time in his life (in the world's life indeed, for before him no man had known it) he tasted — *crackling*! Again he felt and fumbled at the pig. It did not burn him so much now, still he licked his fingers from a sort of habit. The truth at length broke into his slow understanding, that it was the pig that smelt so, and the pig that tasted so delicious; and, surrendering himself up to the newborn pleasure, he fell to tearing up whole handfuls of the scorched skin with the flesh next it, and was cramming it down his throat in his beastly fashion, when his sire entered amid the smoking rafters, armed with retributory cudgel, and finding how affairs stood, began to rain blows upon the young rogue's shoulders, as thick as hailstones, which Bo-bo heeded not any more than if they had been flies. The tickling pleasure, which he experienced in his lower regions, had rendered him quite callous to any inconveniences he might feel in those remote quarters. His father might lay on, but he could not beat him from his pig, till he had fairly made an end of it, when, becoming a little more sensible of his situation, something like the following dialogue ensued.

" You graceless whelp, what have you got there devouring? Is it not enough that you have burnt me down three houses with your dog's tricks, and be hanged to you, but you must be eating fire, and I know not what — what have you got there, I say?"

" O, father, the pig, the pig, do come and taste how nice the burnt pig eats."

The ears of Ho-ti tingled with horror. He cursed his son, and he cursed himself that ever he should beget a son that should eat burnt pig.

Bo-bo, whose scent was wonderfully sharpened since morning, soon raked out another pig, and fairly rending it asunder, thrust the lesser half by main force into the fists of Ho-ti, still shouting out " Eat, eat, eat the burnt pig, father, only taste — O Lord," — with such-like barbarous ejaculations, cramming all the while as if he would choke.

Ho-ti trembled every joint while he grasped the abominable thing, wavering whether he should not put his son to death for an unnatural young monster, when the crackling scorching his fingers, as it had done his son's, and applying the same remedy to them, he in his turn tasted some of its flavour, which, make what sour mouths he would for a pretence, proved not altogether displeasing to him. In conclusion (for the manuscript here is a little tedious) both father and son fairly sat down to the mess, and never left off till they had despatched all that remained of the litter.

Bo-bo was strictly enjoined not to let the secret escape, for the neighbours would certainly have stoned them for a couple of abominable wretches, who could think of improving upon the good meat which God had sent them. Nevertheless, strange stories got about. It was observed that Ho-ti's cottage was burnt down now more frequently than ever. Nothing but fires from this time forward. Some would break out in broad day, others in the night-time. As often as the sow farrowed, so sure was the house of Ho-ti to be in a blaze; and Ho-ti himself, which was the more remarkable, instead of chastising his son, seemed to grow more indulgent to him than ever. At length they were watched, the terrible mystery discovered, and father and son summoned to take their trial at Pekin, then an inconsiderable assize town. Evidence was given, the obnoxious food itself produced in court, and verdict about to be pronounced, when the foreman of the jury begged that some of the burnt pig, of which the culprits stood accused, might be handed into the box. He handled it, and they all handled it, and burning their fingers, as Bo-bo and his father had done before them, and nature prompting to each of them the same remedy, against the face of all the facts, and the clearest charge which judge had ever given, — to the surprise of the whole court, townsfolk, strangers, reporters, and all present — without leaving the box, or any manner of consultation whatever, they brought in a simultaneous verdict of Not Guilty.

The judge, who was a shrewd fellow, winked at the manifest iniquity of the decision; and, when the court was dismissed, went privily, and bought up all the pigs that could be had for love or money. In a few days his Lordship's town house was observed to be on fire. The thing took wing, and now there was nothing to be seen but fires in every direction. Fuel and pigs grew enormously dear all over the district. The insurance offices one and all shut up shop. People built slighter and slighter every day, until it was feared that the very science of architecture would in no long time be lost to the world. Thus this custom of firing houses continued, till in process of time, says my manuscript, a sage arose, like our Locke, who made a discovery, that the flesh of swine, or indeed of any other animal, might be cooked (*burnt*, as they called it) without the necessity of consuming a whole house to dress it. Then first began the rude form of a gridiron. Roasting by the string, or spit, came in a century or two later, I forget in whose dynasty. By such slow degrees, concludes the manuscript, do the most useful, and seemingly the most obvious arts, make their way among mankind. ——

Without placing too implicit faith in the account above given, it must be agreed, that if a worthy pretext for so dangerous an experiment as setting houses on fire (especially in these days) could be assigned in favour of any culinary object, that pretext and excuse might be found in ROAST PIG.

Of all the delicacies in the whole *mundus edibilis*, I will maintain it to be the most delicate — *princeps obsoniorum.*

I speak not of your grown porkers — things between pig and pork — those hobbledehoys — but a young and tender suckling — under a moon old — guiltless as yet of the sty — with no original speck of the *amor immunditiæ*, the hereditary failing of the first parent, yet manifest — his voice as yet not broken, but something between a childish treble, and a grumble — the mild forerunner, or *præludium*, of a grunt.

He must be roasted. I am not ignorant that our ancestors ate them seethed, or boiled — but what a sacrifice of the exterior tegument!

There is no flavour comparable, I will contend, to that of the crisp, tawny, well-watched, not over-roasted, *crackling*, as it is well called — the very teeth are invited to their share of the pleasure at this banquet in overcoming the coy, brittle resistance — with the adhesive oleaginous — O call it not fat — but an indefinable sweetness growing up to it — the tender blossoming of fat — fat cropped in the bud — taken in the shoot — in the first innocence — the cream and quintessence of the child-pig's yet pure food —— the lean, no lean, but a kind of animal manna — or, rather, fat and lean (if it must be so), so blended and running into each other, that both together make but one ambrosian result, or common substance.

Behold him, while he is doing — it seemeth rather a refreshing warmth, than a scorching heat, that he is so passive to. How equably he twirleth round the string! — Now he is just done. To see the extreme sensibility of that tender age, he hath wept out his pretty eyes — radiant jellies — shooting stars —

See him in the dish, his second cradle, how meek he lieth! — wouldst thou have had this innocent grow up to the grossness and indocility which too often accompany maturer swinehood? Ten to one he would have proved a glutton, a sloven, an obstinate, disagreeable animal —

wallowing in all manner of filthy conversation — from these sins he is happily snatched away —

> Ere sin could blight, or sorrow fade,
> Death came with timely care —

his memory is odoriferous — no clown curseth, while his stomach half rejecteth, the rank bacon — no coalheaver bolteth him in reeking sausages — he hath a fair sepulchre in the grateful stomach of the judicious epicure — and for such a tomb might be content to die.

He is the best of Sapors. Pine-apple is great. She is indeed almost too transcendent — a delight, if not sinful, yet so like to sinning, that really a tender-conscienced person would do well to pause — too ravishing for mortal taste, she woundeth and excoriateth the lips that approach her — like lovers' kisses, she biteth — she is a pleasure bordering on pain from the fierceness and insanity of her relish — but she stoppeth at the palate — she meddleth not with the appetite — and the coarsest hunger might barter her consistently for a mutton chop.

Pig — let me speak his praise — is no less provocative of the appetite, than he is satisfactory to the criticalness of the censorious palate. The strong man may batten on him, and the weakling refuseth not his mild juices.

Unlike to mankind's mixed characters, a bundle of virtues and vices, inexplicably intertwisted, and not to be unravelled without hazard, he is — good throughout. No part of him is better or worse than another. He helpeth, as far as his little means extend, all around. He is the least envious of banquets. He is all neighbours' fare.

I am one of those, who freely and ungrudgingly impart a share of the good things of this life which fall to their lot (few as mine are in this kind) to a friend. I protest

I take as great an interest in my friend's pleasures, his
relishes, and proper satisfactions, as in mine own. " Presents," I often say, " endear Absents." Hares, pheasants,
partridges, snipes, barn-door chickens (those " tame
villatic fowl "), capons, plovers, brawn, barrels of oysters,
I dispense as freely as I receive them. I love to taste
them, as it were, upon the tongue of my friend. But a
stop must be put somewhere. One would not, like Lear,
" give everything ". I make my stand upon pig. Methinks it is an ingratitude to the Giver of all good flavours,
to extra-domiciliate, or send out of the house, slightingly
(under pretext of friendship, or I know not what) a
blessing so particularly adapted, predestined, I may say,
to my individual palate — It argues an insensibility.

I remember a touch of conscience in this kind at school.
My good old aunt, who never parted from me at the end
of a holiday without stuffing a sweetmeat, or some nice
thing, into my pocket, had dismissed me one evening
with a smoking plum-cake, fresh from the oven. In my
way to school (it was over London Bridge) a grey-
headed old beggar saluted me (I have no doubt at this
time of day that he was a counterfeit). I had no pence to
console him with, and in the vanity of self-denial, and
the very coxcombry of charity, school-boy-like, I made
him a present of — the whole cake! I walked on a little,
buoyed up, as one is on such occasions, with a sweet
soothing of self-satisfaction; but before I had got to the
end of the bridge, my better feelings returned, and I
burst into tears, thinking how ungrateful I had been to
my good aunt, to go and give her good gift away to a
stranger, that I had never seen before, and who might
be a bad man for aught I knew; and then I thought of
the pleasure my aunt would be taking in thinking that

I — I myself, and not another — would eat her nice cake — and what should I say to her the next time I saw her — how naughty I was to part with her pretty present — and the odour of that spicy cake came back upon my recollection, and the pleasure and the curiosity I had taken in seeing her make it, and her joy when she sent it to the oven, and how disappointed she would feel that I had never had a bit of it in my mouth at last — and I blamed my impertinent spirit of alms-giving, and out-of-place hypocrisy of goodness, and above all I wished never to see the face again of that insidious, good-for-nothing, old grey impostor.

Our ancestors were nice in their method of sacrificing these tender victims. We read of pigs whipt to death with something of a shock, as we hear of any other obsolete custom. The age of discipline is gone by, or it would be curious to inquire (in a philosophical light merely) what effect this process might have towards intenerating and dulcifying a substance, naturally so mild and dulcet as the flesh of young pigs. It looks like refining a violet. Yet we should be cautious, while we condemn the inhumanity, how we censure the wisdom of the practice. It might impart a gusto —

I remember an hypothesis, argued upon by the young students, when I was at St. Omer's, and maintained with much learning and pleasantry on both sides, " Whether, supposing that the flavour of a pig who obtained his death by whipping (*per flagellationem extremam*) superadded a pleasure upon the palate of a man more intense than any possible suffering we can conceive in the animal, is man justified in using that method of putting the animal to death?" I forget the decision.

His sauce should be considered. Decidedly, a few

bread crumbs, done up with his liver and brains, and a dash of mild sage. But, banish, dear Mrs. Cook, I beseech you, the whole onion tribe. Barbecue your whole hogs to your palate, steep them in shalots, stuff them out with plantations of the rank and guilty garlic; you cannot poison them, or make them stronger than they are — but consider, he is a weakling — a flower.

OLD CHINA

I have an almost feminine partiality for old china. When I go to see any great house, I enquire for the china-closet, and next for the picture gallery. I cannot defend the order of preference, but by saying, that we have all some taste or other, of too ancient a date to admit of our remembering distinctly that it was an acquired one. I can call to mind the first play, and the first exhibition, that I was taken to; but I am not conscious of a time when china jars and saucers were introduced into my imagination.

I had no repugnance then — why should I now have? — to those little, lawless, azure-tinctured grotesques, that under the notion of men and women, float about, uncircumscribed by any element, in that world before perspective — a china tea-cup.

I like to see my old friends — whom distance cannot diminish — figuring up in the air (so they appear to our optics), yet on *terra firma* still — for so we must in courtesy interpret that speck of deeper blue, — which the decorous artist, to prevent absurdity, had made to spring up beneath their sandals.

I love the men with women's faces, and the women, if possible, with still more womanish expressions.

Here is a young and courtly Mandarin, handing tea to a lady from a salver — two miles off. See how distance seems to set off respect! And here the same lady, or another — for likeness is identity on tea-cups — is stepping into a little fairy boat, moored on the hither side of this calm garden river, with a dainty mincing foot, which in a right angle of incidence (as angles go in our world) must infallibly land her in the midst of a flowery mead — a furlong off on the other side of the same strange stream!

Farther on — if far or near can be predicated of their world — see horses, trees, pagodas, dancing the hays.

Here — a cow and rabbit couchant, and co-extensive — so objects show, seen through the lucid atmosphere of fine Cathay.

I was pointing out to my cousin last evening, over our Hyson, (which we are old fashioned enough to drink unmixed still of an afternoon) some of these *speciosa miracula* upon a set of extraordinary old blue china (a recent purchase) which we were now for the first time using; and could not help remarking, how favourable circumstances had been to us of late years, that we could afford to please the eye sometimes with trifles of this sort — when a passing sentiment seemed to overshade the brows of my companion. I am quick at detecting these summer clouds in Bridget.

" I wish the good old times would come again," she said, " when we were not quite so rich. I do not mean, that I want to be poor; but there was a middle state " — so she was pleased to ramble on, — " in which I am sure we were a great deal happier. A purchase is but a purchase, now that you have money enough and to spare.

Formerly it used to be a triumph. When we coveted a
cheap luxury (and, O! how much ado I had to get you
to consent in those times!) — we were used to have a de-
bate two or three days before, and to weigh the *for* and
against, and think what we might spare it out of, and
what saving we could hit upon, that should be an equiva-
lent. A thing was worth buying then, when we felt the
money that we paid for it.

" Do you remember the brown suit, which you made to
hang upon you, till all your friends cried shame upon
you, it grew so thread-bare — and all because of that
folio Beaumont and Fletcher, which you dragged home
late at night from Barker's in Covent Garden? Do you
remember how we eyed it for weeks before we could make
up our minds to the purchase, and had not come to a
determination till it was near ten o'clock of the Saturday
night, when you set off from Islington, fearing you
should be too late — and when the old bookseller with
some grumbling opened his shop, and by the twinkling
taper (for he was setting bedwards) lighted out the relic
from his dusty treasures — and when you lugged it home,
wishing it were twice as cumbersome — and when you
presented it to me — and when we were exploring the
perfectness of it (*collating* you called it) — and while I was
repairing some of the loose leaves with paste, which your
impatience would not suffer to be left till daybreak —
was there no pleasure in being a poor man? or can those
neat black clothes, which you wear now, and are so
careful to keep brushed, since we have become rich and
finical, give you half the honest vanity, with which you
flaunted it about in that overworn suit — your old cor-
beau — for four or five weeks longer than you should
have done, to pacify your conscience for the mighty sum

of fifteen — or sixteen shillings was it? — a great affair we thought it then — which you had lavished on the old folio? Now you can afford to buy any book that pleases you, but I do not see that you ever bring me home any nice old purchases now.

" When you came home with twenty apologies for laying out a less number of shillings upon that print after Lionardo, which we christened the ' Lady Blanch '; when you looked at the purchase, and thought of the money — and thought of the money, and looked again at the picture — was there no pleasure in being a poor man? Now, you have nothing to do but to walk into Colnaghi's, and buy a wilderness of Lionardos. Yet do you?

" Then, do you remember our pleasant walks to Enfield, and Potter's Bar, and Waltham, when we had a holyday — holydays, and all other fun, are gone, now we are rich — and the little hand-basket in which I used to deposit our day's fare of savoury cold lamb and salad — and how you would pry about at noon-tide for some decent house, where we might go in, and produce our store — only paying for the ale that you must call for — and speculate upon the looks of the landlady, and whether she was likely to allow us a table-cloth — and wish for such another honest hostess, as Izaak Walton has described many a one on the pleasant banks of the Lea, when he went a fishing — and sometimes they would prove obliging enough, and sometimes they would look grudgingly upon us — but we had cheerful looks still for one another, and would eat our plain food savorily, scarcely grudging Piscator his Trout Hall? Now, — when we go out a day's pleasuring, which is seldom moreover, we *ride* part of the way — and go into a fine inn, and order the best of dinners, never debating the expense —

which, after all, never has half the relish of those chance country snaps, when we were at the mercy of uncertain usage, and a precarious welcome.

" You are too proud to see a play anywhere now but in the pit. Do you remember where it was we used to sit, when we saw the Battle of Hexham, and the Surrender of Calais, and Bannister and Mrs. Bland in the Children in the Wood — when we squeezed out our shillings a-piece to sit three or four times in a season in the one-shilling gallery — where you felt all the time that you ought not to have brought me — and more strongly I felt obligation to you for having brought me — and the pleasure was the better for a little shame — and when the curtain drew up, what cared we for our place in the house, or what mattered it where we were sitting, when our thoughts were with Rosalind in Arden, or with Viola at the Court of Illyria? You used to say, that the Gallery was the best place of all for enjoying a play socially — that the relish of such exhibitions must be in proportion to the infrequency of going — that the company we met there, not being in general readers of plays, were obliged to attend the more, and did attend, to what was going on, on the stage — because a word lost would have been a chasm, which it was impossible for them to fill up. With such reflections we consoled our pride then — and I appeal to you, whether, as a woman, I met generally with less attention and accommodation, than I have done since in more expensive situations in the house? The getting in indeed, and the crowding up those inconvenient staircases, was bad enough, — but there was still a law of civility to woman recognised to quite as great an extent as we ever found in the other passages — and how a little difficulty overcome heightened the snug seat, and

the play, afterwards! Now we can only pay our money
and walk in. You cannot see, you say, in the galleries
now. I am sure we saw, and heard too, well enough then
— but sight, and all, I think, is gone with our poverty.

" There was pleasure in eating strawberries, before
they became quite common — in the first dish of peas,
while they were yet dear — to have them for a nice
supper, a treat. What treat can we have now? If we
were to treat ourselves now — that is, to have dainties a
little above our means, it would be selfish and wicked.
It is the very little more that we allow ourselves beyond
what the actual poor can get at, that makes what I call
a treat — when two people living together, as we have
done, now and then indulge themselves in a cheap luxury,
which both like; while each apologises, and is willing to
take both halves of the blame to his single share. I see
no harm in people making much of themselves in that
sense of the word. It may give them a hint how to
make much of others. But now — what I mean by the
word — we never do make much of ourselves. None but
the poor can do it. I do not mean the veriest poor of all,
but persons as we were, just above poverty.

" I know what you were going to say, that it is mighty
pleasant at the end of the year to make all meet, — and
much ado we used to have every Thirty-first Night of
December to account for our exceedings — many a long
face did you make over your puzzled accounts, and in
contriving to make it out how we had spent so much —
or that we had not spent so much — or that it was impossible we should spend so much next year — and still
we found our slender capital decreasing — but then,
betwixt ways, and projects, and compromises of one sort
or another, and talk of curtailing this charge, and doing

without that for the future — and the hope that youth brings, and laughing spirits (in which you were never poor till now) we pocketed up our loss, and in conclusion, with ' lusty brimmers ' (as you used to quote it out of *hearty cheerful Mr. Cotton*, as you called him), we used to welcome in the ' coming guest '. Now we have no reckoning at all at the end of the old year — no flattering promises about the new year doing better for us."

Bridget is so sparing of her speech on most occasions, that when she gets into a rhetorical vein, I am careful how I interrupt it. I could not help, however, smiling at the phantom of wealth which her dear imagination had conjured up out of a clear income of a poor — hundred pounds a year. " It is true we were happier when we were poorer, but we were also younger, my cousin. I am afraid we must put up with the excess, for if we were to shake the superflux into the sea, we should not much mend ourselves. That we had much to struggle with, as we grew up together, we have reason to be most thankful. It strengthened, and knit our compact closer. We could never have been what we have been to each other, if we had always had the sufficiency which you now complain of. The resisting power — those natural dilations of the youthful spirit, which circumstances cannot straighten — with us are long since passed away. Competence to age is supplementary youth, a sorry supplement indeed, but I fear the best that is to be had. We must ride, where we formerly walked: live better, and lie softer — and shall be wise to do so — than we had means to do in those good old days you speak of. Yet could those days return — could you and I once more walk out thirty miles a-day — could Bannister and Mrs. Bland again be young, and you and I be young to see them — could the good old one-shilling gallery days return — they are dreams, my cousin, now — but could you and I at this moment, instead of this quiet argument, by our well-carpeted fire-side, sitting on this luxurious sofa — be once more struggling up those inconvenient staircases, pushed about, and squeezed, and elbowed by the poorest rabble of poor gallery scramblers — could I once more hear those anxious shrieks of yours — and the delicious *Thank God, we are safe*, which always followed when the topmost stair, conquered, let in the first light of the whole cheerful theatre down beneath us — I know not the fathom line that ever touched a descent so deep as I would be willing to bury more wealth in than Crœsus had, or the great Jew R—— is supposed to have, to purchase it. And now do just look at that merry little Chinese waiter holding an umbrella, big enough for a bed-tester, over the head of that pretty insipid half-Madonnaish chit of a lady in that very blue summer house."

DREAM-CHILDREN: A REVERIE

Children love to listen to stories about their elders, when *they* were children; to stretch their imagination to the conception of a traditionary great-uncle or grandame, whom they never saw. It was in this spirit that my little ones crept about me the other evening to hear about their great-grandmother Field, who lived in a great house in Norfolk (a hundred times bigger than that in which they and papa lived) which had been the scene — so at least it was generally believed in that part of the country — of the tragic incidents which they had lately become familiar with from the ballad of the Children in the Wood. Certain it is that the whole story of the children and their cruel uncle was to be seen fairly carved out in wood upon the chimney-piece of the great hall, the whole story down to the Robin Redbreasts, till a foolish rich person pulled it down to set up a marble one of modern invention in its stead, with no story upon it. Here Alice put out one of her dear mother's looks, too tender to be called upbraiding. Then I went on to say, how religious and how good their great-grandmother Field was, how beloved and respected by everybody, though she was not indeed the mistress of this great house, but had only the charge of it (and yet in some respects she might be said to be the mistress of it too) committed to her by the owner, who preferred living in a newer and more fashionable mansion which he had purchased somewhere in the adjoining county; but still she lived in it in a manner as if it had been her own, and kept up the dignity of the great house in a sort while she lived, which afterwards came to decay, and was nearly pulled down, and all its old ornaments stripped and carried away to the owner's other house, where they were set up, and looked as awkward as if some one were to carry away the old tombs they had seen lately at the Abbey, and stick them up in Lady C.'s tawdry gilt drawing-room. Here John smiled, as much as to say, " that would be foolish indeed ". And then I told how, when she came to die, her funeral was attended by a concourse of all the poor, and some of the gentry too, of the neighbourhood for many miles round, to show their respect for her memory, because she had been such a good and religious woman; so good indeed that she knew all the Psaltery by heart, ay, and a great part of the Testa-

ment besides.   Here little Alice spread her hands.
Then I told what a tall, upright, graceful person their
great-grandmother Field once was; and how in her
youth she was esteemed the best dancer — here Alice's
little right foot played an involuntary movement, till
upon my looking grave, it desisted — the best dancer, I
was saying, in the county, till a cruel disease, called a
cancer, came, and bowed her down with pain; but it
could never bend her good spirits, or make them stoop,
but they were still upright, because she was so good and
religious.   Then I told how she was used to sleep by
herself in a lone chamber of the great lone house; and
how she believed that an apparition of two infants was
to be seen at midnight gliding up and down the great
staircase near where she slept, but she said " those
innocents would do her no harm;" and how frightened
I used to be, though in those days I had my maid to
sleep with me, because I was never half so good or religious as she — and yet I never saw the infants.   Here
John expanded all his eyebrows and tried to look coura-
geous.   Then I told how good she was to all her grand-
children, having us to the great house in the holydays,
where I in particular used to spend many hours by myself,
in gazing upon the old busts of the Twelve Cæsars, that
had been Emperors of Rome, till the old marble heads
would seem to live again, or I to be turned into marble
with them; how I never could be tired with roaming
about that huge mansion, with its vast empty rooms, with
their worn-out hangings, fluttering tapestry, and carved
oaken panels, with the gilding almost rubbed out — sometimes in the spacious old-fashioned gardens, which I had
almost to myself, unless when now and then a solitary
gardening man would cross me — and how the nec-

tarines and peaches hung upon the walls, without my
ever offering to pluck them, because they were forbidden
fruit, unless now and then, — and because I had more
pleasure in strolling about among the old melancholy-
looking yew trees, or the firs, and picking up the red
berries, and the fir apples, which were good for nothing
but to look at — or in lying about upon the fresh grass,
with all the fine garden smells around me — or basking
in the orangery, till I could almost fancy myself ripening
too along with the oranges and the limes in that grateful
warmth — or in watching the dace that darted to and
fro in the fish-pond, at the bottom of the garden, with
here and there a great sulky pike hanging midway down
the water in silent state, as if it mocked at their impertinent friskings, — I had more pleasure in these busy-idle
diversions than in all the sweet flavours of peaches, nec-
tarines, oranges, and such like common baits of children.
Here John slyly deposited back upon the plate a bunch
of grapes, which, not unobserved by Alice, he had meditated dividing with her, and both seemed willing to
relinquish them for the present as irrelevant.   Then in
somewhat a more heightened tone, I told how, though
their great-grandmother Field loved all her grand-
children, yet in an especial manner she might be said
to love their uncle, John L——, because he was so handsome and spirited a youth, and a king to the rest of us;
and, instead of moping about in solitary corners, like
some of us, he would mount the most mettlesome horse
he could get, when but an imp no bigger than themselves,
and make it carry him half over the county in a morning,
and join the hunters when there were any out — and yet
he loved the old great house and gardens too, but had
too much spirit to be always pent up within their boun-

daries — and how their uncle grew up to man's estate as
brave as he was handsome, to the admiration of every
body, but of their great-grandmother Field most especially; and how he used to carry me upon his back when
I was a lame-footed boy — for he was a good bit older
than me — many a mile when I could not walk for pain;
— and how in after life he became lame-footed too, and
I did not always (I fear) make allowances enough for him
when he was impatient, and in pain, nor remember
sufficiently how considerate he had been to me when I
was lame-footed; and how, when he died, though he
had not been dead an hour, it seemed as if he had died
a great while ago, such a distance there is betwixt life and
death; and how I bore his death as I thought pretty well
at first, but afterwards it haunted and haunted me; and
though I did not cry or take it to heart as some do, and
as I think he would have done if I had died, yet I missed
him all day long, and knew not till then how much I had
loved him.   I missed his kindness, and I missed his
crossness, and wished him to be alive again, to be quar-
relling with him (for we quarrelled sometimes), rather
than not have him again, and was as uneasy without him,
as he their poor uncle must have been when the doctor
took off his limb.   Here the children fell a crying, and
asked if their little mourning which they had on was not
for uncle John, and they looked up, and prayed me not to
go on about their uncle, but to tell them some stories
about their pretty dead mother.   Then I told how for
seven long years, in hope sometimes, sometimes in
despair, yet persisting ever, I courted the fair Alice
W———n; and, as much as children could understand, I
explained to them what coyness, and difficulty, and
denial meant in maidens — when suddenly, turning to

Alice, the soul of the first Alice looked out at her eyes with such a reality of re-presentment, that I became in doubt which of them stood there before me, or whose that bright hair was; and while I stood gazing, both the children gradually grew fainter to my view, receding, and still receding till nothing at last but two mournful features were seen in the uttermost distance, which, without speech, strangely impressed upon me the effects of speech; "We are not of Alice, nor of thee, nor are we children at all. The children of Alice call Bartrum father. We are nothing; less than nothing, and dreams. We are only what might have been, and must wait upon the tedious shores of Lethe millions of ages before we have existence, and a name " — and immediately awaking, I found myself quietly seated in my bachelor armchair, where I had fallen asleep, with the faithful Bridget unchanged by my side — but John L. (or James Elia) was gone for ever.

WILLIAM HAZLITT

(1778–1830)

Hazlitt, born three years after Lamb, was as erratic and hot-tempered as Lamb was gentle and placid. At his best, he is brilliant; but his work is very uneven. The description of John Cavanagh which follows (it is an excerpt from a much longer essay on Indian Jugglers) is one of his greatest passages. His work has often a vividness which is sometimes lacking in that of Lamb; but he in turn lacks the emotional powers of Lamb. His opinions are always strongly expressed. Of his life, it is enough to say that he was, like Goldsmith, the son of a minister, and was himself destined for the Church, but turned to painting instead, and forsook that for literature and literary criticism. His life was passed in a series of quarrels with almost all who knew him.

JOHN CAVANAGH

" Died at his house in Burbage Street, St. Giles's, John Cavanagh, the famous hand fives-player. When a person dies who does any one thing better than any one else in the world, which so many others are trying to do well, it leaves a gap in society. It is not likely that any one will now see the game of fives played in its perfection for many years to come — for Cavanagh is dead, and has not left his peer behind him. It may be said that there are things of more importance than striking a ball against a wall — there are things, indeed, that make more noise and do as little good, such as making war and peace, making speeches and answering

them, making verses and blotting them, making money
and throwing it away. But the game of fives is what
no one despises who has ever played at it. It is the
finest exercise for the body, and the best relaxation for
the mind. The Roman poet said that ' Care mounted
behind the horseman and stuck to his skirts '. But
this remark would not have applied to the fives-player.
He who takes to playing at fives is twice young. He feels
neither the past nor future ' in the instant '. Debts,
taxes, ' domestic treason, foreign levy, nothing can touch
him further '. He has no other wish, no other thought,
from the moment the game begins, but that of striking
the ball, of placing it, of *making* it! This Cavanagh was
sure to do. Whenever he touched the ball there was an
end of the chase. His eye was certain, his hand fatal, his
presence of mind complete. He could do what he
pleased, and he always knew exactly what to do. He
saw the whole game, and played it; took instant advantage of his adversary's weakness, and recovered
balls, as if by a miracle and from sudden thought, that
every one gave for lost. He had equal power and skill,
quickness and judgment. He could either outwit his
antagonist by finesse, or beat him by main strength.
Sometimes, when he seemed preparing to send the ball
with the full swing of his arm, he would by a slight
turn of his wrist drop it within an inch of the line. In
general, the ball came from his hand, as if from a racket,
in a straight, horizontal line; so that it was in vain to
attempt to overtake or stop it. As it was said of a great
orator that he never was at a loss for a word, and for the
properest word, so Cavanagh always could tell the degree
of force necessary to be given to a ball, and the precise
direction in which it should be sent. He did his work

with the greatest ease; never took more pains than was necessary; and while others were fagging themselves to death, was as cool and collected as if he had just entered the court. His style of play was as remarkable as his power of execution. He had no affectation, no trifling. He did not throw away the game to show off an attitude or try an experiment. He was a fine, sensible, manly player, who did what he could, but that was more than any one else could even affect to do. His blows were not undecided and ineffectual — lumbering like Mr. Wordsworth's epic poetry, nor wavering like Mr. Coleridge's lyric prose, nor short of the mark like Mr. Brougham's speeches, nor wide of it like Mr. Canning's wit, nor foul like the *Quarterly*, nor *let* balls like the *Edinburgh Review*. Cobbett and Junius together would have made a Cavanagh. He was the best *up-hill* player in the world; even when his adversary was fourteen, he would play on the same or better, and as he never flung away the game through carelessness and conceit, he never gave it up through laziness or want of heart. The only peculiarity of his play was that he never *volleyed*, but let the balls hop; but if they rose an inch from the ground he never missed having them. There was not only nobody equal, but nobody second to him. It is supposed that he could give any other player half the game, or beat them with his left hand. His service was tremendous. He once played Woodward and Meredith together (two of the best players in England) in the Fives-court, St. Martin's Street, and made seven-and-twenty aces following by services alone — a thing unheard of. He another time played Peru, who was considered a first-rate fives-player, a match of the best out of five games, and in the three first games, which *of*

course decided the match, Peru got only one ace. Cavanagh was an Irishman by birth, and a house-painter by
profession. He had once laid aside his working-dress,
and walked up, in his smartest clothes, to the Rosemary
branch to have an afternoon's pleasure. A person ac-
costed him, and asked him if he would have a game. So
they agreed to play for half-a-crown a game and a bottle
of cider. The first game began — it was seven, eight,
ten, thirteen, fourteen, all. Cavanagh won it. The next
was the same. They played on, and each game was hardly
contested. 'There,' said the unconscious fives-player,
'there was a stroke that Cavanagh could not take: I never
played better in my life, and yet I can't win a game.
I don't know how it is!' However, they played on,
Cavanagh winning every game, and the bystanders
drinking the cider and laughing all the time. In the
twelfth game, when Cavanagh was only four, and the
stranger thirteen, a person came in and said, 'What!
are you here, Cavanagh?' The words were no sooner
pronounced than the astonished player let the ball drop
from his hand, and saying, 'What! have I been breaking my heart all this time to beat Cavanagh?' refused
to make another effort. 'And yet, I give you my word,'
said Cavanagh, telling the story with some triumph,
'I played all the while with my clenched fist.' He used
frequently to play matches at Copenhagen House for
wagers and dinners. The wall against which they play
is the same that supports the kitchen-chimney, and when
the wall resounded louder than usual, the cooks exclaimed, 'Those are the Irishman's balls,' and the joints
trembled on the spit! Goldsmith consoled himself that
there were places where he too was admired: and Cavanagh was the admiration of all the fives-courts where

he ever played. Mr. Powell, when he played matches in
the court in St. Martin's Street, used to fill his gallery
at half-a-crown a head with amateurs and admirers of
talent in whatever department it is shown. He could not
have shown himself in any ground in England but he
would have been immediately surrounded with inquisi-
tive gazers, trying to find out in what part of his frame
his unrivalled skill lay, as politicians wonder to see the
balance of Europe suspended in Lord Castlereagh's face,
and admire the trophies of the British Navy lurking under
Mr. Croker's hanging brow. Now Cavanagh was as
good-looking a man as the Noble Lord, and much better
looking than the Right Hon. Secretary. He had a clear,
open countenance, and did not look sideways or down,
like Mr. Murray the bookseller. He was a young fellow
of sense, humour, and courage. He once had a quarrel
with a waterman at Hungerford Stairs, and, they say,
served him out in great style. In a word, there are hun-
dreds at this day who cannot mention his name without
admiration, as the best fives-player that perhaps ever
lived (the greatest excellence of which they have any
notion); and the noisy shout of the ring happily stood
him in stead of the unheard voice of posterity! — The
only person who seems to have excelled as much in
another way as Cavanagh did in his was the late John
Davies, the racket-player. It was remarked of him that
he did not seem to follow the ball, but the ball seemed
to follow him. Give him a foot of wall, and he was sure
to make the ball. The four best racket-players of that
day were Jack Spines, Jem Harding, Armitage, and
Church. Davies could give any one of these two hands a
time, that is, half the game, and each of these, at their
best, could give the best player now in London the same

odds. Such are the gradations in all exertions of human skill and art. He once played four capital players together, and beat them. He was also a first-rate tennis-player, and an excellent fives-player. In the Fleet or King's Bench he would have stood against Powell, who was reckoned the best open-ground player of his time. This last-mentioned player is at present the keeper of the Fives-court, and we might recommend to him for a motto over his door, ' Who enters here, forgets himself, his country, and his friends'. And the best of it is, that by the calculation of the odds, none of the three are worth remembering! Cavanagh died from the bursting of a blood-vessel, which prevented him from playing for the last two or three years. This, he was often heard to say, he thought hard upon him. He was fast recovering, however, when he was suddenly carried off, to the regret of all who knew him. As Mr. Peel made it a qualification of the present Speaker, Mr. Manners Sutton, that he was an excellent moral character, so Jack Cavanagh was a zealous Catholic, and could not be persuaded to eat meat on a Friday, the day on which he died. We have paid this willing tribute to his memory.

> Let no rude hand deface it,
> And his forlorn ' *Hic Jacet* '."

ON FAMILIAR STYLE

It is not easy to write a familiar style. Many people mistake a familiar for a vulgar style, and suppose that to write without affectation is to write at random. On the contrary, there is nothing that requires more precision, and, if I may so say, purity of expression, than the style I am speaking of. It utterly rejects not only all unmeaning pomp, but all low, cant phrases, and loose, unconnected, *slipshod* allusions. It is not to take the first word that offers, but the best word in common use; it is not to throw words together in any combinations we please, but to follow and avail ourselves of the true idiom of the language. To write a genuine familiar or truly English style is to write as any one would speak in common conversation who had a thorough command and choice of words, or who could discourse with ease, force, and perspicuity, setting aside all pedantic and oratorical flourishes. Or, to give another illustration, to write naturally is the same thing in regard to common conversation as to read naturally is in regard to common speech. It does not follow that it is an easy thing to give the true accent and inflection to the words you utter, because you do not attempt to rise above the level of ordinary life and colloquial speaking. You do not assume, indeed, the solemnity of the pulpit, or the tone of stage-declamation; neither are you at liberty to gabble on at a venture, without emphasis or discretion, or to resort to vulgar dialect or clownish pronunciation. You must steer a middle course. You are tied down to a given and appropriate articulation, which is determined by the habitual associations between sense and sound, and which you can only hit by entering into the author's meaning, as you must find the proper words and style to express yourself by fixing your thoughts on the subject you have to write about. Any one may mouth out a passage with a theatrical cadence, or get upon stilts to tell his thoughts; but to write or speak with propriety and simplicity is a more difficult task. Thus it is easy to affect a pompous style, to use a word twice as big as the thing you want to express: it is not so easy to pitch upon the very word that exactly fits it. Out of eight or ten words equally common, equally intelligible, with nearly equal pretensions, it is a matter of some nicety and discrimination to pick out the very one the preferableness of which is scarcely perceptible, but decisive. The reason why I object to Dr. Johnson's style is that there is no discrimination, no selection, no variety in it. He uses none but " tall, opaque words ", taken from the " first row of the rubric " — words with the greatest number of syllables, or Latin phrases with merely English terminations. If a fine style depended on this sort of arbitrary pretension, it would be fair to judge of an author's elegance by the measurement of his words and the substitution of foreign circumlocutions (with no precise associations) for the mother-tongue.[1] How simple is it to be dignified without ease, to be pompous without meaning! Surely it is but a mechanical rule for avoiding what is low, to be always pedantic and affected. It is clear you cannot use a vulgar English word if you never use a common English word at all. A fine tact is shown in adhering to those which are perfectly common, and yet never falling into any expressions which are debased by disgusting circumstances, or which owe their signification and point to technical or professional allusions. A truly natural or familiar style can never be quaint or vulgar, for this reason, that it is of universal force and applicability, and that quaintness and vulgarity arise out of

---

[1] I have heard of such a thing as an author who makes it a rule never to admit a monosyllable into his vapid verse. Yet the charm and sweetness of Marlowe's lines depended often on their being made up almost entirely of monosyllables.

the immediate connection of certain words with coarse and disagreeable or with confined ideas. The last form what we understand by *cant* or *slang* phrases. — To give an example of what is not very clear in the general statement. I should say that the phrase *To cut with a knife*, or *To cut a piece of wood*, is perfectly free from vulgarity, because it is perfectly common; but to *cut an acquaintance* is not quite unexceptionable, because it is not perfectly common or intelligible, and has hardly yet escaped out of the limits of slang phraseology. I should hardly, therefore, use the word in this sense without putting it in italics as a license of expression, to be received *cum grano salis*. All provincial or bye-phrases come under the same mark of reprobation — all such as the writer transfers to the page from his fireside or a particular *coterie*, or that he invents for his own sole use and convenience. I conceive that words are like money, not the worse for being common, but that it is the stamp of custom alone that gives them circulation or value. I am fastidious in this respect, and would almost as soon coin the currency of the realm as counterfeit the King's English. I never invented or gave a new and unauthorised meaning to any word but one single one (the term *impersonal* applied to feelings), and that was in an abstruse metaphysical discussion to express a very difficult distinction. I have been (I know) loudly accused of revelling in vulgarisms and broken English. I cannot speak to that point; but so far I plead guilty to the determined use of acknowledged idioms and common elliptical expressions. I am not sure that the critics in question know the one from the other, that is, can distinguish any medium between formal pedantry and the most barbarous solecism. As an author I endeavour to employ plain words and popular modes of construction, as, were I a chapman and dealer, I should common weights and measures.

The proper force of word lies not in the words themselves, but in their application. A word may be a fine-sounding word, of an unusual length, and very imposing from its learning and novelty, and yet in the connection in which it is introduced may be quite pointless and irrelevant. It is not pomp or pretension, but the adaptation of the expression to the idea, that clenches a writer's meaning: — as it is not the size or glossiness of the materials, but their being fitted each to its place, that gives strength to the arch; or as the pegs and nails are as necessary to the support of the building as the larger timbers, and more so than the mere showy, unsubstantial ornaments. I hate anything that occupies more space than it is worth. I hate to see a load of bandboxes go along the street, and I hate to see a parcel of big words without anything in them. A person who does not deliberately dispose of all his thoughts alike in cumbrous draperies and flimsy disguises may strike out twenty varieties of familiar everyday language, each coming somewhat nearer to the feeling he wants to convey, and at last not hit upon that particular and only one which may be said to be identical with the exact impression in his mind. This would seem to show that Mr. Cobbett is hardly right in saying that the first word that occurs is always the best. It may be a very good one; and yet a better may present itself on reflection or from time to time. It should be suggested naturally, however, and spontaneously, from a fresh and lively conception of the subject. We seldom succeed by trying at improvement, or by merely substituting one word for another that we are not satisfied with, as we cannot recollect the name of a place or person by merely plaguing ourselves about it. We wander farther from the point by persisting in a wrong scent; but it starts up accidentally in the memory when we least expected it, by touching some link in the chain of previous association.

There are those who hoard up and make a cautious display of nothing but rich and rare phraseology — ancient medals, obscure coins, and Spanish pieces of eight. They are very curious to inspect, but I myself would neither offer nor take them in the course of exchange. A sprinkling of archaisms is not amiss, but a tissue of obsolete expressions is more fit *for keep than wear*. I do not say I would not use any phrase that had been brought into fashion before the middle or the end of the last century, but I should be shy of using any that had not been employed by any approved author during the whole of that time. Words, like clothes, get old-fashioned, or mean and ridiculous, when they have been for some time laid aside. Mr. Lamb is the only imitator of old English style I can read with pleasure; and he is so thoroughly imbued with the spirit of his authors that the idea of imitation is almost done away. There is an inward unction, a marrowy vein, both in the thought and feeling, an intuition, deep and lively, of his subject, that carries off any quaintness or awkwardness arising from an antiquated style and dress. The matter is completely his own, though the manner is assumed. Perhaps his ideas are altogether so marked and individual as to require their point and pungency to be neutralised by the affectation of a singular but traditional form of conveyance. Tricked out in the prevailing costume,

they would probably seem more startling and out of
the way. The old English authors, Burton, Fuller,
Coryate, Sir Thomas Browne, are a kind of mediators
between us and the more eccentric and whimsical
modern, reconciling us to his peculiarities. I do not,
however, know how far this is the case or not, till he
condescends to write like one of us. I must confess
that what I like best of his papers under the signature
of Elia (still I do not presume, amidst such excellence,
to decide what is most excellent) is the account of " Mrs.
Battle's Opinions on Whist ", which is also the most free
from obsolete allusions and turns of expression —

A well of native English undefiled.

To those acquainted with his admired prototypes,
these *Essays* of the ingenious and highly gifted author
have the same sort of charm and relish that Erasmus's
Colloquies or a fine piece of modern Latin have to the
classical scholar. Certainly, I do not know any borrowed
pencil that has more power or felicity of execution than
the one of which I have here been speaking.

It is as easy to write a gaudy style without ideas as
it is to spread a pallet of showy colours or to smear
in a flaunting transparency. " What do you read?"
" Words, words, words." — " What is the matter?"
" *Nothing*," it might be answered. The florid style is
the reverse of the familiar. The last is employed as
an unvarnished medium to convey ideas; the first is
resorted to as a spangled veil to conceal the want of
them. When there is nothing to be set down but words,
it costs little to have them fine. Look through the dictionary, and cull out a *florilegium*, rival the *tulippomania*.
Rouge high enough, and never mind the natural com-

plexion. The vulgar, who are not in the secret, will admire the look of preternatural health and vigour; and the fashionable, who regard only appearances, will be delighted with the imposition. Keep to your sounding generalities, your tinkling phrases, and all will be well. Swell out an unmeaning truism to a perfect tympany of style. A thought, a distinction is the rock on which all this brittle cargo of verbiage splits at once. Such writers have merely *verbal* imaginations, that retain nothing but words. Or their puny thoughts have dragon-wings, all green and gold. They soar far above the vulgar failing of the *Sermo humi obrepens* — their most ordinary speech is never short of an hyperbole, splendid, imposing, vague, incomprehensible, magniloquent, a cento of sounding common-places. If some of us, whose " ambition is more lowly ", pry a little too narrowly into nooks and corners to pick up a number of " unconsidered trifles ", they never once direct their eyes or lift their hands to seize on any but the most gorgeous, tarnished, threadbare, patchwork set of phrases, the left-off finery of poetic extravagance, transmitted down through successive generations of barren pretenders. If they criticise actors and actresses, a huddled phantasmagoria of feathers, spangles, floods of light, and oceans of sound float before their morbid sense, which they paint in the style of Ancient Pistol. Not a glimpse can you get of the merits or defects of the performers: they are hidden in a profusion of barbarous epithets and wilful rhodomontade. Our hypercritics are not thinking of these little fantoccini beings —

That strut and fret their hour upon the stage —

but of tall phantoms of words, abstractions, *genera*

and *species*, sweeping clauses, periods that unite the
Poles, forced alliterations, astounding antitheses —

And on their pens *Fustian* sits plumed.

If they describe kings and queens, it is an Eastern
pageant. The Coronation at either House is nothing
to it. We get at four repeated images — a curtain, a
throne, a sceptre, and a footstool. These are with them
the wardrobe of a lofty imagination; and they turn
their servile strains to servile uses. Do we read a description of pictures? It is not a reflection of tones and
hues which "nature's own sweet and cunning hand
laid on", but piles of precious stones, rubies, pearls,
emeralds, Golconda's mines, and all the blazonry of
art. Such persons are in fact besotted with words, and
their brains are turned with the glittering but empty
and sterile phantoms of things. Personifications, capital
letters, seas of sunbeams, visions of glory, shining in-
scriptions, the figures of a transparency, Britannia with
her shield, or Hope leaning on an anchor, make up their
stock-in-trade. They may be considered as *hieroglyphi-
cal* writers. Images stand out in their minds isolated
and important merely in themselves, without any ground-
work of feeling — there is no context in their imaginations. Words affect them in the same way, by the mere
sound, that is, by their possible, not by their actual
application to the subject in hand. They are fascinated
by first appearances, and have no sense of consequences.
Nothing more is meant by them than meets the ear:
they understand or feel nothing more than meets their
eye. The web and texture of the universe, and of the
heart of man, is a mystery to them: they have no faculty
that strikes a chord in unison with it. They cannot get

beyond the daubings of fancy, the varnish of sentiment. Objects are not linked to feelings, words to things, but images revolve in splendid mockery, words represent themselves in their strange rhapsodies. The categories of such a mind are pride and ignorance — pride in outside show, to which they sacrifice everything, and ignorance of the true worth and hidden structure both of words and things. With a sovereign contempt for what is familiar and natural, they are the slaves of vulgar affectation — of a routine of high-flown phrases. Scorning to imitate realities, they are unable to invent anything, to strike out one original idea. They are not copyists of nature, it is true; but they are the poorest of all plagiarists, the plagiarists of words. All is far-fetched, dear-bought, artificial, oriental in subject and allusion; all is mechanical, conventional, vapid, formal, pedantic in style and execution. They startle and confound the understanding of the reader by the remoteness and obscurity of their illustrations; they soothe the ear by the monotony of the same everlasting round of circuitous metaphors. They are the *mock-school* in poetry and prose. They flounder about between fustian in expression and bathos in sentiment. They tantalise the fancy, but never reach the head nor touch the heart. Their Temple of Fame is like a shadowy structure raised by Dulness to Vanity, or like Cowper's description of the Empress of Russia's palace of ice, " as worthless as in show 'twas glittering " ——

It smiled, and it was cold!

JAMES LEIGH HUNT

(1784–1859)

Like Goldsmith and Hazlitt, Leigh Hunt was the son of a minister; like Hazlitt, he was in the habit of expressing his opinions with more freedom than tact; like Lamb, he stammered; and he was as haphazard and unpractical as Goldsmith. Even in his own day, he was a very minor light in the literary world; yet he was a master of the light essay, and his easy style makes very pleasant reading.

ON THE GRACES AND ANXIETIES OF PIG-DRIVING

From the perusal of this article we beg leave to warn off vulgar readers of all denominations, whether of the " great vulgar or the small ". Warn, did we say? We drive them off; for Horace tells us that they, as well as pigs, are to be so treated. *Odi profanum vulgus,* says he, *et arceo.* But do thou lend thine ear, gentle shade of Goldsmith, who didst make thy bear-leader denounce " everything as is low "; and thou, Steele, who didst humanise upon public-houses and puppet-shows; and Fielding, thou whom the great Richardson, less in that matter (and some others) than thyself, did accuse of vulgarity, because thou didst discern natural gentility in a footman, and yet was not to be taken in by the airs of Pamela and my Lady G.

The title is a little startling; but " style and sentiment ", as a lady said, " can do anything ". Remember, then, gentle reader, that talents are not to be despised in the humblest walks of life; we will add, nor in the muddiest. The other day we happened to be among a set of spectators who could not help stopping to admire the patience and address with which a pig-driver huddled and cherished onward his drove of unaccommodating *élèves*, down a street in the suburbs. He was a born genius for a manœuvre. Had he originated in a higher sphere he would have been a general, or a stage-manager, or, at least, the head of a set of monks. Conflicting interests were his forte; pig-headed wills, and proceedings hopeless. To see the *hand* with which he did it! How hovering, yet firm; how encouraging, yet compelling; how indicative of the space on each side of him, and yet of the line before him; how general, how particular, how perfect! No barber's could quiver about a head with more lightness of apprehension; no cook's pat up and proportion the side of a pasty with a more final eye. The whales, quoth old Chapman, speaking of Neptune,

The whales exulted under him, and knew their mighty king.

The pigs did not exult, but they knew their king. Unwilling was their subjection, but " more in sorrow than in anger ". They were too far gone for rage. Their case was hopeless. They did not see why they should proceed, but they felt themselves bound to do so; forced, conglomerated, crowded onwards, irresistibly impelled by fate and Jenkins. Often would they have bolted under any other master. They squeaked and grunted as in ordinary; they sidled, they shuffled, they half stopped; they turned an eye to all the little outlets of escape; but in vain. There they stuck (for their very progress was a sort of sticking), charmed into the centre of his sphere of action, laying their heads together, but to no purpose; looking all as if they were shrugging their shoulders, and eschewing the tip-end of the whip of office. Much eye had they to their left leg; shrewd backward glances; not a little anticipative squeak and sudden rush of avoidance. It was a superfluous clutter, and they felt it; but a pig finds it more difficult than any other animal to accommodate himself to circumstances. Being out of his pale, he is in the highest state of wonderment and inaptitude. He is sluggish, obstinate, opinionate, not very social; has no desire of seeing foreign parts. Think of him in a multitude, forced to travel, and wondering what the devil it is that drives him! Judge by this of the talents of his driver.

We beheld a man once, an inferior genius, inducting a pig into the other end of Long Lane, Smithfield. He had got him thus far towards the market. It was much. His air announced success in nine parts out of ten, and hope for the remainder. It had been a happy morning's work; he had only to look for the termination of it; and he looked (as a critic of an exalted turn of mind would say) in brightness and in joy. Then would he go to the public-house, and indulge in porter and a pleasing security. Perhaps he would not say much at first, being oppressed with the greatness of his success; but by degrees, especially if interrogated, he would open, like Æneas, into all the circumstances of his journey and the perils that beset him. Profound would be his set out; full of tremor his middle course; high and skilful his progress; glorious, though with a quickened pulse, his triumphant entry. Delicate had been his situation in Ducking Pond Row; masterly his turn at Bell Alley. We saw him with the radiance of some such thought on his countenance. He was just entering Long Lane. A gravity came upon him, as he steered his touchy convoy into his last thoroughfare. A dog moved him into a little agitation, darting along; but he resumed his course, not without a happy trepidation, hovering as he was on the borders of triumph. The pig still required care. It was evidently a pig with all the peculiar turn of mind of his species; a fellow that would not move faster than he could help; irritable, retrospective; picking objections, and prone to boggle; a chap with a tendency to take every path but the proper one, and with a sidelong tact for the alleys.

He bolts!

He's off! — *Evasit! erupit!*

"Oh," exclaimed the man, dashing his hand against his head, lifting his knee in an agony, and screaming with all the weight of a prophecy which the spectators felt to be too true — "*He'll go up all manner of streets!*"

Poor fellow! we think of him now sometimes, driving up Duke Street, and not to be comforted in Barbican.

ON GETTING UP ON COLD MORNINGS

An Italian author — Giulio Cordara, a Jesuit — has written a poem upon insects, which he begins by insisting, that those troublesome and abominable little animals were created for our annoyance, and that they were certainly not inhabitants of Paradise. We of the north may dispute this piece of theology; but on the other hand, it is as clear as the snow on the house-tops, that Adam was not under the necessity of shaving; and that when Eve walked out of her delicious bower, she did not step upon ice three inches thick.

Some people say it is a very easy thing to get up of a cold morning. You have only, they tell you, to take the resolution; and the thing is done. This may be very true; just as a boy at school has only to take a flogging, and the thing is over. But we have not at all made up our minds upon it; and we find it a very pleasant exercise to discuss the matter, candidly, before we get up. This, at least, is not idling, though it may be lying. It affords an excellent answer to those who ask how lying in bed can be indulged in by a reasoning being, — a rational creature. How? Why, with the argument calmly at work in one's head, and the clothes over one's shoulder. Oh — it is a fine way of spending a sensible impartial half-hour.

If these people would be more charitable they would get on with their argument better. But they are apt to reason so ill, and to assert so dogmatically, that one could wish to have them stand round one's bed, of a bitter morning, and *lie* before their faces. They ought to hear both sides of the bed, the inside and out. If they cannot entertain themselves with their own thoughts for half-an-hour or so, it is not the fault of those who can.

Candid inquiries into one's decumbency, besides the greater or less privileges to be allowed a man in proportion to his ability of keeping early hours, the work given his faculties, etc., will at least concede their due merits to such representations as the following. In the first place, says the injured but calm appealer, I have been warm all night, and find my system in a state perfectly suitable to a warm-blooded animal. To get out of this state into the cold, besides the inharmonious and uncritical abruptness of the transition, is so unnatural to such a creature, that the poets, refining upon the tortures of the damned, make one of their greatest agonies consist in being suddenly transported from heat to cold, — from fire to ice. They are " haled out " of their " beds ", says Milton, by " harpy-footed furies ", — fellows who come to call them. On my first movement towards the anticipation of getting up I find that such parts of the sheets and bolster as are exposed to the air of the room are stone-cold. On opening my eyes, the first thing that meets them is my own breath rolling forth, as if in the open air, like smoke out of a chimney. Think of this symptom. Then I turn my eyes sideways and see the window all frozen over. Think of that. Then the servant comes in. " It is very cold this morning, is it not?" — " Very cold, sir." — " Very cold indeed, isn't it?" — " Very cold indeed, sir." — " More than usually so, isn't it, even for this weather?" (Here the servant's wit and good-nature are put to a considerable test, and the inquirer lies on thorns for the answer.) " Why, sir . . . I think it *is*." (Good creature! There is not a better or more truth-telling servant going.) " I must rise, however — get me some warm water." — Here comes a fine interval between the departure of the servant and the arrival of the hot water; during which, of course, it is of " no use?" to get up. The hot water comes. " Is it quite hot?" — " Yes, sir." — " Perhaps too hot for shaving; I must wait a little?" — " No, sir; it will just do." (There is an over-nice propriety sometimes, an officious zeal of virtue, a little troublesome.) " Oh — the shirt — you must air my clean shirt; — linen gets very damp this weather." — " Yes, sir." Here another delicious five minutes. A knock at the door. " Oh, the shirt — very well. My stockings — I think the stockings had better be aired too." — " Very well,

sir." Here another interval. At length everything is
ready, except myself. I now, continues our incumbent (a
happy word, by-the-by, for a country vicar) — I now
cannot help thinking a good deal — who can? — upon
the unnecessary and villainous custom of shaving: it
is a thing so unmanly (here I nestle closer) — so effemi-
nate (here I recoil from an unlucky step into the colder
part of the bed). — No wonder that the Queen of France
took part with the rebels against that degenerate king,
her husband, who first affronted her smooth visage with
a face like her own. The Emperor Julian never showed
the luxuriancy of his genius to better advantage than in
reviving the flowing beard. Look at Cardinal Bembo's
picture — at Michael Angelo's — at Titian's — at Shakespeare's — at Fletcher's — at Spenser's — at Chaucer's
— at Alfred's — at Plato's — I could name a great man
for every tick of my watch. — Look at the Turks, a
grave and otiose people. — Think of Haroun Al Raschid
and Bed-ridden Hassan. — Think of Wortley Mon-
tague, the worthy son of his mother, above the prejudice
of his time. — Look at the Persian gentlemen, whom one
is ashamed of meeting about the suburbs, their dress and
appearance are so much finer than our own. — Lastly,
think of the razor itself — how totally opposed to every
sensation of bed — how cold, how edgy, how hard!
how utterly different from anything like the warm and
circling amplitude, which

> Sweetly recommends itself
> Unto our gentle senses.

Add to this, benumbed fingers, which may help you
to cut yourself, a quivering body, a frozen towel, and
a ewer full of ice; and he that says there is nothing

to oppose in all this, only shows that he has no merit in opposing it.

Thomson the poet, who exclaims in his *Seasons* —

Falsely luxurious! Will not man awake?

used to lie in bed till noon, because he said he had no motive in getting up. He could imagine the good of rising; but then he could also imagine the good of lying still; and his exclamation, it must be allowed, was made upon summer-time, not winter. We must proportion the argument to the individual character. A money-getter may be drawn out of his bed by three or four pence; but this will not suffice for a student. A proud man may say, "What shall I think of myself, if I don't get up?" but the more humble one will be content to waive this prodigious notion of himself, out of respect to his kindly bed. The mechanical man shall get up without any ado at all; and so shall the barometer. An ingenious lier in bed will find hard matter of discussion even on the score of health and longevity. He will ask us for our proofs and precedents of the ill effects of lying later in cold weather; and sophisticate much on the advantages of an even temperature of body; of the natural propensity (pretty universal) to have one's way; and of the animals that roll themselves up and sleep all the winter. As to longevity, he will ask whether the longest is of necessity the best; and whether Holborn is the handsomest street in London.

THOMAS DE QUINCEY

(1785–1859)

De Quincey, the son of a wealthy father, was born in Manchester in 1785. After an erratic boyhood, during which he ran away from school and wandered about Wales and London, he went to Oxford, where he met Wordsworth and Coleridge. From the latter he acquired the habit of taking opium, a habit that remained with him all his life, but which we probably have to thank, in part at least, for his extraordinarily vivid power of description. The essay which follows is one of his greatest. It is also a splendid example of literary criticism.

ON THE KNOCKING AT THE GATE IN MACBETH

From my boyish days I had always felt a great perplexity on one point in Macbeth: it was this: the knocking at the gate, which succeeds to the murder of Duncan, produced to my feelings an effect for which I never could account: the effect was — that it reflected back upon the murder a peculiar awfulness and a depth of solemnity: yet, however obstinately I endeavoured with my understanding to comprehend this, for many years I never could see *why* it should produce such an effect. ——

Here I pause for one moment to exhort the reader never to pay any attention to his understanding when it stands in opposition to any other faculty of his mind. The mere understanding, however useful and indispensable, is the meanest faculty in the human mind and the most to be distrusted: and yet the great majority of people trust to nothing else; which may do for ordinary life, but not for philosophic purposes. Of this, out of ten thousand instances that I might produce, I will cite one. Ask of any person whatsoever, who is not previously prepared for the demand by a knowledge of perspective, to draw in the rudest way the commonest appearance which depends upon the laws of that science — as for instance, to represent the effect of two walls standing at right angles to each other, or the appearance of the houses on each side of a street, as seen by a person looking down the street from one extremity. Now in all cases, unless the person has happened to observe in pictures how it is that artists produce these effects, he will be utterly unable to make the smallest approximation to it. Yet why? — For he has actually seen the effect every day of his life. The reason is — that he allows his understanding to overrule his eyes. His understanding, which includes no intuitive knowledge of the laws of vision, can furnish him with no reason why a line which is known and can be proved to be a horizontal line, should not *appear* a horizontal line: a line, that made any angle with the perpendicular less than a right angle, would seem to him to indicate that his houses were all tumbling down together. Accordingly he makes the line of his houses a horizontal line, and fails of course to produce the effect demanded. Here then is one instance out of many, in which not only the understanding is allowed to overrule the eyes, but where the understanding is positively allowed to obliterate the eyes as it were: for not only does the man believe the evidence of his understanding in opposition to that of his eyes, but (which is monstrous!) the idiot is not aware that his eyes ever gave such evidence. He does not know that he has seen (and therefore *quoad* his consciousness has *not* seen) that which he *has* seen every day of his life. But to return from this digression, — my understanding could furnish no reason why the knocking at the gate in Macbeth should produce any effect direct or reflected: in fact, my understanding said positively that it could *not* produce any effect. But I knew better: I felt that it did: and I waited and clung to the problem until further knowledge should enable me to solve it. — At length, in 1812, Mr. Williams made his *début* on the stage of Ratcliffe Highway, and executed those unparalleled murders which have procured for him such a brilliant and undying reputation. On which murders, by the way, I must observe, that in one respect they have had an ill effect, by making the connoisseur in murder very fastidious in his taste, and dissatisfied with any thing that has been since done in that line. All other murders look pale by the deep crimson of his: and, as an amateur once said to me in a querulous tone, " There has been absolutely nothing *doing* since his time, or nothing that's worth speaking of." But this is wrong: for it is unreasonable to expect all men to be great artists, and born with the genius of Mr. Williams. — Now it will be remembered that in the first of these murders (that of the Marrs) the same incident (of a knocking at the door soon after the work of extermination was complete) did actually occur which the genius of Shakspeare had invented: and all good judges and the most eminent dilettanti acknowledged the felicity of Shakspeare's suggestion as soon as it was actually realized. Here then was a fresh proof that I had been right in relying on my own feeling in opposition to my understanding; and again I set myself to study the problem: at length I solved it to my own satisfaction; and my solution is this. Murder in ordinary cases, where the sympathy is wholly directed to the case of the murdered person, is an incident of coarse and vulgar horror; and for this reason — that it flings the interest exclusively upon the natural but ignoble instinct by which we cleave to life; an instinct which, as being indispensable to the primal law of self-preservation, is the same in kind (though different in degree) amongst all living creatures; this instinct therefore, because it annihilates all distinctions, and degrades the greatest of men to the level of "the poor beetle that we tread on", exhibits human nature in its most abject and humiliating attitude. Such an attitude would little suit the purposes of the poet. What then must he do? He must throw the interest on the murderer: our sympathy must be with *him*; (of course I mean a sympathy of comprehension, a sympathy by which we enter into his feelings, and are made to understand them, — not a sympathy [1] of pity or approbation:) in the murdered person all strife of thought, all flux and reflux of passion and of purpose, are crushed by one overwhelming panic: the fear of instant death smites him "with its petrific mace". But in the murderer, such a murderer as a poet will condescend to, there must be raging some great storm of passion, — jealousy, ambition, vengeance, hatred, — which will create a hell within him; and into this hell we are to look. In Macbeth, for the sake of

---

[1] It seems almost ludicrous to guard and explain my use of a word in a situation where it should naturally explain itself. But it has become necessary to do so, in consequence of the unscholarlike use of the word sympathy, at present so general, by which, instead of taking it in its proper use, as the act of reproducing in our minds the feelings of another, whether for hatred, indignation, love, pity, or approbation, it is made a mere synonyme of the word *pity*; and hence, instead of saying, "sympathy *with* another", many writers adopt the monstrous barbarism of "sympathy *for* another".

gratifying his own enormous and teeming faculty of creation, Shakspeare has introduced two murderers: and, as usual in his hands, they are remarkably discriminated: but though in Macbeth the strife of mind is greater than in his wife, the tiger spirit not so awake, and his feelings caught chiefly by contagion from her, — yet, as both were finally involved in the guilt of murder, the murderous mind of necessity is finally to be presumed in both. This was to be expressed; and on its own account, as well as to make it a more proportionable antagonist to the unoffending nature of their victim, " the gracious Duncan ", and adequately to expound " the deep damnation of his taking off ", this was to be expressed with peculiar energy. We were to be made to feel that the human nature, i.e. the divine nature of love and mercy, spread through the hearts of all creatures, and seldom utterly withdrawn from man, — was gone, vanished, extinct; and that the fiendish nature had taken its place. And, as this effect is marvellously accomplished in the dialogues and soliloquies themselves, so it is finally consummated by the expedient under consideration; and it is to this that I now solicit the reader's attention. If the reader has ever witnessed a wife, daughter, or sister, in a fainting fit, he may chance to have observed that the most affecting moment in such a spectacle, is *that* in which a sigh and a stirring announce the recommencement of suspended life. Or, if the reader has ever been present in a vast metropolis on the day when some great national idol was carried in funeral pomp to his grave, and chancing to walk near to the course through which it passed, has felt powerfully in the silence and desertion of the streets and in the stagnation of ordinary business, the deep interest which at that moment was possessing the heart of man, — if all at once he should hear the death-like stillness broken up by the sound of wheels rattling away from the scene, and making known that the transitory vision was dissolved, he will be aware that at no moment was his sense of the complete suspension and pause in ordinary human concerns so full and affecting as at that moment when the suspension ceases, and the goings-on of human life are suddenly resumed. All action in any direction is best expounded, measured, and made apprehensible, by reaction. Now apply this to the case in Macbeth. Here, as I have said, the retiring of the human heart and the entrance of the fiendish heart was to be expressed and made sensible. Another world has stepped in; and the murderers are taken out of the region of human things, human purposes, human desires. They are transfigured: Lady Macbeth is " unsexed "; Macbeth has forgot that he was born of woman; both are conformed to the image of devils; and the world of devils is suddenly revealed. But how shall this be conveyed and made palpable? In order that a new world may step in, this world must for a time disappear. The murderers, and the murder, must be insulated — cut off by an immeasurable gulph from the ordinary tide and succession of human affairs — locked up and sequestered in some deep recess: we must be made sensible that the world of ordinary life is suddenly arrested — laid asleep — tranced — racked into a dread armistice: time must be annihilated; relation to things without abolished; and all must pass self-withdrawn into a deep syncope and suspension of earthly passion. Hence it is that when the deed is done — when the work of darkness is perfect, then the world of darkness passes away like a pageantry in the clouds: the knocking at the gate is heard; and it makes known audibly that the reaction has commenced: the human has made its reflux upon the fiendish: the pulses of life are beginning to beat again: and the re-establishment of the goings-on of the world in which we live, first makes us profoundly sensible of the awful parenthesis that had suspended them.

Oh! mighty poet! — Thy works are not as those of other men, simply and merely great works of art; but are also like the phenomena of nature, like the sun and the sea, the stars and the flowers, — like frost and snow, rain and dew, hail-storm and thunder, which are to be studied with entire submission of our own faculties, and in the perfect faith that in them there can be no too much or too little, nothing useless or inert — but that, the further we press in our discoveries, the more we shall see proofs of design and self-supporting arrangement where the careless eye had seen nothing but accident!

N.B. In the above specimen of psychological criticism, I have purposely omitted to notice another use of the knocking at the gate, viz. the opposition and contrast which it produces in the porter's comments to the scenes immediately preceding; because this use is tolerably obvious to all who are accustomed to reflect on what they read.

THOMAS CARLYLE

(1795–1881)

Thomas Carlyle was born in Ecclefechan, Dumfriesshire, of poor but admirable parents. Naturally precocious, he was well educated, at first with a view to the ministry; but he became a schoolmaster instead. From this he turned to literary work, and in 1834 settled down in London, already an established writer. The remainder of his long and rather melancholy life was spent in London. He is important in the world of literature for his powerful if sometimes harsh style and his marked individuality. The essay which follows will give a good idea of both these qualities. His greatest work is probably his *French Revolution*, a remarkable work which he termed a prose epic, and which is quite unlike any other work in the English language.

SIR JABESH WINDBAG

Oliver Cromwell, whose body they hung on their Tyburn gallows because he had found the Christian Religion inexecutable in this country, remains to me by far the remarkablest Governor we have had here for the last five centuries or so. For the last five centuries, there has been no Governor among us with anything like similar talent; and for the last two centuries, no Governor, we may say, with the possibility of similar talent, — with an idea in the heart of him capable of inspiring similar talent, capable of co-existing therewith. When you consider that Oliver believed in a God, the difference between Oliver's position and that of any subsequent Governor of this Country becomes, the more you reflect on it, the more immeasurable!

Oliver, no volunteer in Public Life, but plainly a balloted soldier strictly ordered thither, enters upon Public Life; comports himself there like a man who carried his own life in his hand; like a man whose Great Commander's eye was always on him. Not without results. Oliver, well-advanced in years, finds now, by Destiny and his own Deservings, or as he himself better phrased it, by wondrous successive " Births of Providence ", the Government of England put into his hands. In senate-house and battle-field, in counsel and in action, in private and in public, this man has proved himself a man: England and the voice of God, through waste awful whirlwinds and environments, speaking to his great heart, summon him to assert formally, in the way of solemn Public Fact and as a new piece of English Law, what informally and by Nature's eternal Law needed no asserting. That he, Oliver, was the Ablest Man of England, the King of England; that he, Oliver, would undertake governing England. His way of making this same " assertion ", the one way he had of making it, has given rise to immense criticism: but the assertion itself, in what way soever " made ", is it not somewhat of a solemn one, somewhat of a tremendous one!

And now do but contrast this Oliver with my right honourable friend Sir Jabesh Windbag, Mr. Facing-both-ways, Viscount Mealymouth, Earl of Windlestraw, or what other Cagliostro, Cagliostrino, Cagliostraccio, the course of Fortune and Parliamentary Majorities has constitutionally guided to that dignity, any time during these last sorrowful hundred-and-fifty years! Windbag, weak in the faith of a God, which he believes only at

Church on Sundays, if even then; strong only in the faith that Paragraphs and Plausibilities bring votes; that Force of Public Opinion, as he calls it, is the primal Necessity of Things, and highest God we have: — Windbag, if we will consider him, has a problem set before him which may be ranged in the impossible class. He is a Columbus minded to sail to the indistinct country of NOWHERE, to the indistinct country of WHITHERWARD, by the *friendship* of those same waste-tumbling Water-Alps and howling waltz of All the Winds; not by conquest of them and in spite of them, but by friendship of them, when once *they* have made-up their mind! He is the most original Columbus I ever saw. Nay, his problem is not an impossible one: he will infallibly *arrive* at that same country of NOWHERE; his indistinct Whitherward will be a *Thither*ward! In the Ocean Abysses and Locker of Davy Jones, there certainly enough do he and *his* ship's company, and all their cargo and navigatings, at last find lodgment.

Oliver knew that his America lay THERE. Westward ho; — and it was not entirely by *friendship* of the Water-Alps, and yeasty insane Froth-Oceans, that he meant to get thither! He sailed accordingly; had compass-card, and Rules of Navigation, — older and greater than these Froth-Oceans, old as the Eternal God! Or again, do but think of this. Windbag in these his probable five years of office has to prosper and get Paragraphs: the Paragraphs of these five years must be his salvation, or he is a lost man; redemption nowhere in the Worlds or in the Times discoverable for him. Oliver too would like his Paragraphs; successes, popularities in these five years are not undesirable to him: but mark, I say, this enormous circumstance: *after* these five years are gone and done, comes an Eternity for Oliver! Oliver has to appear before the Most High Judge: the utmost flow of Paragraphs, the utmost ebb of them, is now, in strictest arithmetic, verily no matter at all; its exact value *zero*; an account altogether erased! Enormous: — which a man, in these days, hardly fancies with an effort! Oliver's Paragraphs are all done, his battles, division-lists, successes all summed: and now in that awful unerring Court of Review, the real question first rises, Whether he has succeeded at all; whether he has not been defeated miserably forevermore? Let him come with world-wide *Io-Paeans*, these avail him not. Let him come covered over with the world's execrations, gashed with ignominious death-wounds, the gallows-rope about his neck: what avails that? The word is, Come thou brave and faithful; the word is, Depart thou quack and accursed!

O Windbag, my right honourable friend, in very truth I pity thee. I say, these Paragraphs, and low or loud votings of thy poor fellow-blockheads of mankind, will never guide thee in any enterprise at all. Govern a country on such guidance? Thou canst not make a pair of shoes, sell a pennyworth of tape, on such. No, thy shoes are vamped up falsely to meet the market; behold, the leather only *seemed* to be tanned; thy shoes melt under me to rubbishy pulp, and are not veritable mud-defying shoes, but plausible vendible similitudes of shoes, — thou unfortunate, and I! O my right honour-able friend, when the Paragraphs flowed in, who was like Sir Jabesh? On the swelling tide he mounted; higher, higher, triumphant, heaven-high. But the Para-graphs again ebbed out, as unwise Paragraphs needs must: Sir Jabesh lies stranded, sunk and forever sink-ing in ignominious ooze; the Mud-nymphs, and ever-deepening bottomless Oblivion, his portion to eternal time. " Posterity?" Thou appealest to Posterity, thou? My right honourable friend, what will Posterity do for thee! The voting of Posterity, were it continued through centuries in thy favour, will be quite inaudible, extra-forensic, without any effect whatever. Posterity can do simply nothing for a man; nor even seem to do much if the man be not brainsick. Besides, to tell the truth, the bets are a thousand to one, Posterity will not hear of thee, my right honourable friend! Posterity, I have found, has generally his own windbags sufficiently trumpeted in all market-places, and no leisure to attend to ours. Posterity, which has made of Norse Odin a similitude, and of Norman William a brute monster, what will or can it make of English Jabesh? O Heavens, " Posterity!" —

" These poor persecuted Scotch Covenanters," said I to my inquiring Frenchman, in such stinted French as stood at command, " *ils s'en appelaient à* " — " *A la Postérité*," interrupted he, helping me out. — " *Ah, Monsieur, non, mille fois non!* They appealed to the Eternal God; not to Posterity at all! *C'était différent.*"

THOMAS BABINGTON MACAULAY

(1800–1859)

Macaulay, who was born in London, was very well educated, and proved to be a man of remarkable ability. He was the fortunate possessor of a phenomenal memory, and advanced rapidly in his chosen profession of the law. For his services to the country in Parliament he was raised to the peerage in 1857. His literary reputation rests mainly on his work as a historian, but he wrote many brilliant critical essays. His prose is always vivid, though his accuracy is sometimes questioned. He had a habit of assuming that the facts retained by his own extraordinary memory were equally familiar to all his readers. As well as prose he wrote several poems on historical subjects, which were, however, of only very moderate poetic merit, though they make spirited reading.

OLIVER GOLDSMITH

Oliver Goldsmith, one of the most pleasing English writers of the eighteenth century. He was of a Protestant and Saxon family which had been long settled in Ireland, and which had, like most other Protestant and Saxon families, been, in troubled times, harassed and put in fear by the native population. His father, Charles Goldsmith, studied in the reign of Queen Anne at the diocesan school at Elphin, became attached to the daughter of the schoolmaster, married her, took orders, and settled at a place called Pallas, in the county of Longford. There he with difficulty supported his wife and children on what he could earn, partly as a curate and partly as a farmer.

At Pallas Oliver Goldsmith was born in November 1728. That spot was then, for all practical purposes, almost as remote from the busy and splendid capital in which his later years were passed, as any clearing in Upper Canada or any sheep-walk in Australasia now is. Even at this day those enthusiasts who venture to make a pilgrimage to the birthplace of the poet are forced to perform the latter part of their journey on foot. The hamlet lies far from any highroad on a dreary plain which in wet weather is often a lake. The lanes would break any jaunting-car to pieces; and there are ruts and sloughs through which the most strongly-built wheels cannot be dragged.

While Oliver was still a child, his father was presented to a living worth about £200 a year, in the county of West Meath. The family accordingly quitted their cottage in the wilderness for a spacious house on a frequented road, near the village of Lissoy. Here the boy was taught his letters by a maid-servant, and was sent in his seventh year to a village school kept by an old quarter-master on half-pay, who professed to teach nothing but reading, writing, and arithmetic, but who had an inexhaustible fund of stories about ghosts, banshees, and fairies, about the great Rapparee chiefs, Baldearg O'Donnell and galloping Hogan, and about the exploits of Peterborough and Stanhope, the surprise of Monjuich, and the glorious disaster of Brihuega. This man must have been of the Protestant religion; but he was of the aboriginal race, and not only spoke the Irish language, but could pour forth unpremeditated Irish verses. Oliver early became, and through life continued to be, a passionate admirer of the Irish music, and especially of the compositions of Carolan, some of the last notes of whose harp he heard. It ought to be added that Oliver, though by birth one of the Englishry, and though connected by numerous ties with the Established Church, never showed the least sign of that contemptuous antipathy with which, in his days, the ruling minority in Ireland too generally regarded the subject majority. So far indeed was he from sharing the opinions and feelings of the caste to which he belonged, that he conceived an aversion to the Glorious and Immortal Memory, and, even when George the Third was on the throne, maintained that nothing but the restoration of the banished dynasty could save the country.

From the humble academy kept by the old soldier Goldsmith was removed in his ninth year. He went to several grammar-schools, and acquired some knowledge of the ancient languages. His life at this time seems to have been far from happy. He had, as appears from the admirable portrait of him at Knowle, features harsh even to ugliness. The small-pox had set its mark on him with more than usual severity. His stature was small, and his limbs ill put together. Among boys little tenderness is shown to personal defects; and the ridicule excited by poor Oliver's appearance was heightened by a peculiar simplicity and a disposition to blunder which he retained to the last. He became the common butt of boys and masters, was pointed at as a fright in the playground, and flogged as a dunce in the schoolroom. When he had risen to eminence, those who had once derided him ransacked their memory for the events of his early years, and recited repartees and couplets which had dropped from him, and which, though little noticed at the time, were supposed a quarter of a century later, to indicate the powers which produced the *Vicar of Wakefield* and the *Deserted Village*.

In his seventeenth year Oliver went up to Trinity College, Dublin, as a sizar. The sizars paid nothing for food and tuition, and very little for lodging; but they had to perform some menial services from which they have long been relieved. They swept the court: they carried up the dinner to the fellows' tables, and changed the plates and poured out the ale of the rulers of the society. Goldsmith was quartered, not alone, in a garret, on the window of which his name, scrawled by himself, is still read with interest.[1] From such garrets many men of less parts than his have made their way to the woolsack or to the episcopal bench. But Goldsmith, while he suffered all the humiliations, threw away all the advantages of his situation. He neglected the studies of the place, stood low at the examinations, was turned down to the bottom of his class for playing the buffoon in the lecture-room, was severely reprimanded for pumping on a constable, and was caned by a brutal tutor for giving a ball in the attic story of the college to some gay youths and damsels from the city.

While Oliver was leading at Dublin a life divided between squalid distress and squalid dissipation, his father died, leaving a mere pittance. The youth obtained his bachelor's degree, and left the University. During some time the humble dwelling to which his widowed mother had retired was his home. He was now in his twenty-first year; it was necessary that he

---

[1] The glass on which the name is written has, as we are informed by a writer in *Notes and Queries* (2nd S. ix. p. 91), been enclosed in a frame deposited in the Manuscript Room of the College Library, where it is still to be seen.

should do something; and his education seemed to have fitted him to do nothing but to dress himself in gaudy colours, of which he was as fond as a magpie, to take a hand at cards, to sing Irish airs, to play the flute, to angle in summer, and to tell ghost stories by the fire in winter. He tried five or six professions in turn without success. He applied for ordination; but, as he applied in scarlet clothes, he was speedily turned out of the episcopal palace. He then became tutor in an opulent family, but soon quitted his situation in consequence of a dispute about play. Then he determined to emigrate to America. His relations, with much satisfaction, saw him set out for Cork on a good horse, with thirty pounds in his pocket. But in six weeks he came back on a miserable hack, without a penny, and informed his mother that the ship in which he had taken his passage, having got a fair wind while he was at a party of pleasure, had sailed without him. Then he resolved to study the law. A generous kinsman advanced fifty pounds. With this sum Goldsmith went to Dublin, was enticed into a gaming-house, and lost every shilling. He then thought of medicine. A small purse was made up; and in his twenty-fourth year he was sent to Edinburgh. At Edinburgh he passed eighteen months in nominal attendance on lectures, and picked up some superficial information about chemistry and natural history. Thence he went to Leyden, still pretending to study physic. He left that celebrated university, the third university at which he had resided, in his twenty-seventh year, without a degree, with the merest smattering of medical knowledge, and with no property but his clothes and his flute. His flute, however, proved a useful friend. He rambled on foot through Flanders,

France, and Switzerland, playing tunes which everywhere set the peasantry dancing, and which often procured for him a supper and a bed. He wandered as far
as Italy. His musical performances, indeed, were not to
the taste of the Italians, but he contrived to live on the
alms which he obtained at the gates of convents. It
should, however, be observed that the stories which he
told about this part of his life ought to be received with
great caution; for strict veracity was never one of his
virtues; and a man who is ordinarily inaccurate in nar-
ration is likely to be more than ordinarily inaccurate
when he talks about his own travels. Goldsmith, indeed,
was so regardless of truth as to assert in print that he
was present at a most interesting conversation between
Voltaire and Fontenelle, and that this conversation
took place at Paris. Now it is certain that Voltaire never
was within a hundred leagues of Paris during the whole
time which Goldsmith passed on the Continent.

In 1756 the wanderer landed at Dover, without a
shilling, without a friend, and without a calling. He
had, indeed, if his own unsupported evidence may be
trusted, obtained from the University of Padua a
doctor's degree; but this dignity proved utterly useless to him. In England his flute was not in request;
there were no convents; and he was forced to have
recourse to a series of desperate expedients. He turned
strolling player; but his face and figure were ill suited
to the boards even of the humblest theatre. He pounded
drugs and ran about London with phials for charitable
chemists. He joined a swarm of beggars, which made
its nest in Axe Yard. He was for a time usher of a school,
and felt the miseries and humiliations of this situation
so keenly that he thought it a promotion to be permitted

to earn his bread as a bookseller's hack; but he soon found the new yoke more galling than the old one, and was glad to become an usher again. He obtained a medical appointment in the service of the East India Company: but the appointment was speedily revoked. Why it was revoked we are not told. The subject was one on which he never liked to talk. It is probable that he was incompetent to perform the duties of the place. Then he presented himself at Surgeons' Hall for examination, as mate to a naval hospital. Even to so humble a post he was found unequal. By this time the schoolmaster whom he had served for a morsel of food and the third part of a bed was no more. Nothing remained but to return to the lowest drudgery of literature. Goldsmith took a garret in a miserable court, to which he had to climb from the brink of Fleet Ditch by a dizzy ladder of flagstones called Breakneck Steps. The court and the ascent have long disappeared; but old Londoners will remember both. Here, at thirty, the unlucky adventurer sat down to toil like a galley slave.

In the succeeding six years he sent to the press some things which have survived and many which have perished. He produced articles for reviews, magazines, and newspapers; children's books which, bound in gilt paper and adorned with hideous woodcuts, appeared in the window of the once far-famed shop at the corner of Saint Paul's Churchyard; *An Enquiry into the State of Polite Learning in Europe*, which, though of little or no value, is still reprinted among his works; a *Life of Beau Nash*, which is not reprinted, though it well deserves to be so; a superficial and incorrect, but very readable, *History of England*, in a series of letters purporting to be addressed by a nobleman to his son;

and some lively and amusing *Sketches of London Society*, in a series of letters purporting to be addressed by a Chinese traveller to his friends. All these works were anonymous; but some of them were well known to be Goldsmith's; and he gradually rose in the estimation of the booksellers for whom he drudged. He was, indeed, emphatically a popular writer. For accurate research or grave disquisition he was not well qualified by nature or by education. He knew nothing accurately: his reading had been desultory; nor had he meditated deeply on what he had read. He had seen much of the world; but he had noticed and retained little more of what he had seen than some grotesque incidents and characters which had happened to strike his fancy. But, though his mind was very scantily stored with materials, he used what materials he had in such a way as to produce a wonderful effect. There have been many greater writers; but perhaps no writer was ever more uniformly agreeable. His style was always pure and easy, and, on proper occasions, pointed and energetic. His narratives were always amusing, his descriptions always picturesque, his humour rich and joyous, yet not without an occasional tinge of amiable sadness. About everything that he wrote, serious or sportive, there was a certain natural grace and decorum, hardly to be expected from a man a great part of whose life had been passed among thieves and beggars, street-walkers, and merry-andrews, in those squalid dens which are the reproach of great capitals.

As his name gradually became known, the circle of his acquaintance widened. He was introduced to Johnson, who was then considered as the first of living English writers; to Reynolds, the first of English painters; and to Burke, who had not yet entered Parliament, but who had distinguished himself greatly by his writings and by the eloquence of his conversation. With these eminent men Goldsmith became intimate. In 1763 he was one of the nine original members of that celebrated fraternity which has sometimes been called the Literary Club, but which has always disclaimed that epithet, and still glories in the simple name of The Club.

By this time Goldsmith had quitted his miserable dwelling at the top of Breakneck Steps, and had taken chambers in the more civilized region of the Inns of Court. But he was still often reduced to pitiable shifts. Towards the close of 1764 his rent was so long in arrear that his landlady one morning called in the help of a sheriff's officer. The debtor, in great perplexity, dispatched a messenger to Johnson; and Johnson, always friendly, though often surly, sent back the messenger with a guinea, and promised to follow speedily. He came, and found that Goldsmith had changed the guinea, and was railing at the landlady over a bottle of Madeira. Johnson put the cork into the bottle, and entreated his friend to consider calmly how money was to be procured. Goldsmith said that he had a novel ready for the press. Johnson glanced at the manuscript, saw that there were good things in it, took it to a bookseller, sold it for £60, and soon returned with the money. The rent was paid; and the sheriff's officer withdrew. According to one story, Goldsmith gave his landlady a sharp reprimand for her treatment of him: according to another, he insisted on her joining him in a bowl of punch. Both stories are probably true. The novel which was thus ushered into the world was the *Vicar of Wakefield.*

But, before the *Vicar of Wakefield* appeared in print, came the great crisis of Goldsmith's literary life. In Christmas week, 1764, he published a poem entitled the *Traveller*. It was the first work to which he had put his name; and it at once raised him to the rank of a legitimate English classic. The opinion of the most skilful critics was, that nothing finer had appeared in verse since the fourth book of the *Dunciad*. In one respect the *Traveller* differs from all Goldsmith's other writings. In general his designs were bad, and his execution good. In the *Traveller*, the execution, though deserving of much praise, is far inferior to the design. No philosophical poem, ancient or modern, has a plan so noble, and at the same time so simple. An English wanderer, seated on a crag among the Alps, near the point where three great countries meet, looks down on the boundless prospect, reviews his long pilgrimage, recalls the varieties of scenery, of climate, of government, of religion, of national character, which he has observed, and comes to the conclusion, just or unjust, that our happiness depends little on political institutions, and much on the temper and regulation of our own minds.

While the fourth edition of the *Traveller* was on the counters of the booksellers, the *Vicar of Wakefield* appeared, and rapidly obtained a popularity which has lasted down to our own time, and which is likely to last as long as our language. The fable is indeed one of the worst that ever was constructed. It wants, not merely that probability which ought to be found in a tale of common English life, but that consistency which ought to be found even in the wildest fiction about witches, giants, and fairies. But the earlier chapters have all the sweetness of pastoral poetry, together with all the vivacity of comedy. Moses and his spectacles, the vicar and his monogamy, the sharper and his cosmogony, the squire proving from Aristotle that relatives are related, Olivia preparing herself for the arduous task of converting a rakish lover by studying the controversy between Robinson Crusoe and Friday, the great ladies with their scandal about Sir Tomkyn's amours and Dr. Burdock's verses, and Mr. Burchell with his " Fudge ", have caused as much harmless mirth as has ever been caused by matter packed into so small a number of pages. The latter part of the tale is unworthy of the beginning. As we approach the catastrophe, the absurdities lie thicker and thicker; and the gleams of pleasantry become rarer and rarer.

The success which had attended Goldsmith as a novelist emboldened him to try his fortune as a dramatist. He wrote the *Goodnatured Man*, a piece which had a worse fate than it deserved. Garrick refused to produce it at Drury Lane. It was acted at Covent Garden in 1768, but was coldly received. The author, however, cleared by his benefit nights, and by the sale of the copyright, no less than £500, five times as much as he had made by the *Traveller* and the *Vicar of Wakefield* together. The plot of the *Goodnatured Man* is, like almost all Goldsmith's plots, very ill constructed. But some passages are exquisitely ludicrous; much more ludicrous, indeed, than suited the taste of the town at that time. A canting, mawkish play, entitled *False Delicacy*, had just had an immense run. Sentimentality was all the mode. During some years, more tears were shed at comedies than at tragedies; and a pleasantry which moved the audience to anything more than a grave smile was reprobated as low. It is not strange, therefore, that

the very best scene in the *Goodnatured Man*, that in
which Miss Richland finds her lover attended by the
bailiff and the bailiff's follower in full court dresses,
should have been mercilessly hissed, and should have
been omitted after the first night.

In 1770 appeared the *Deserted Village*. In mere diction and versification this celebrated poem is fully equal,
perhaps superior, to the *Traveller*, and it is generally
preferred to the *Traveller* by that large class of readers
who think, with Bayes in the *Rehearsal*, that the only
use of a plan is to bring in fine things. More discerning
judges, however, while they admire the beauty of the
details, are shocked by one unpardonable fault which
pervades the whole. The fault we mean is not that
theory about wealth and luxury which has so often been
censured by political economists. The theory is indeed
false; but the poem, considered merely as a poem, is
not necessarily the worse on that account. The finest
poem in the Latin language, indeed the finest didactic
poem in any language, was written in defence of the
silliest and meanest of all systems of natural and moral
philosophy. A poet may easily be pardoned for reasoning ill; but he cannot be pardoned for describing ill, for
observing the world in which he lives so carelessly
that his portraits bear no resemblance to the originals,
for exhibiting as copies from real life monstrous combinations of things which never were and never could
be found together. What would be thought of a painter
who should mix August and January in one landscape,
who should introduce a frozen river into a harvest scene?
Would it be a sufficient defence of such a picture to say
that every part was exquisitely coloured, that the green
hedges, the apple-trees loaded with fruit, the wagons

reeling under the yellow sheaves, and the sunburned reapers wiping their foreheads, were very fine, and that the ice and the boys sliding were also very fine? To such a picture the *Deserted Village* bears a great resemblance. It is made up of incongruous parts. The village in its happy days is a true English village. The village in its decay is an Irish village. The felicity and the misery which Goldsmith has brought close together belong to two different countries, and to two different stages in the progress of society. He had assuredly never seen in his native island such a rural paradise, such a seat of plenty, content, and tranquillity, as his " Auburn ". He had assuredly never seen in England all the inhabitants of such a paradise turned out of their homes in one day and forced to emigrate in a body to America. The hamlet he had probably seen in Kent; the ejectment he had probably seen in Munster; but, by joining the two, he has produced something which never was and never will be seen in any part of the world.

In 1773 Goldsmith tried his chance at Covent Garden with a second play, *She Stoops to Conquer*. The manager was not without great difficulty induced to bring this piece out. The sentimental comedy still reigned; and Goldsmith's comedies were not sentimental. The *Goodnatured Man* had been too funny to succeed; yet the mirth of the *Goodnatured Man* was sober when compared with the rich drollery of *She Stoops to Conquer*, which is, in truth, an incomparable farce in five acts. On this occasion, however, genius triumphed. Pit, boxes, and galleries were in a constant roar of laughter. If any bigoted admirer of Kelly and Cumberland ventured to hiss or groan, he was speedily silenced by a general cry

of " Turn him out ", or " Throw him over ". Two
generations have since confirmed the verdict which was
pronounced on that night.

While Goldsmith was writing the *Deserted Village*
and *She Stoops to Conquer*, he was employed in works
of a very different kind, works from which he derived
little reputation but much profit. He compiled for
the use of schools a *History of Rome*, by which he made
£300; a *History of England*, by which he made £600;
a *History of Greece*, for which he received £250; a *Natural
History*, for which the booksellers covenanted to pay
him 800 guineas. These works he produced without
any elaborate research, by merely selecting, abridging,
and translating into his own clear, pure, and flowing
language what he found in books well known to the
world, but too bulky or too dry for boys and girls. He
committed some strange blunders; for he knew nothing
with accuracy. Thus in his *History of England* he tells
us that Naseby is in Yorkshire; nor did he correct this
mistake when the book was reprinted. He was very
nearly hoaxed into putting into the *History of Greece*
an account of a battle between Alexander the Great and
Montezuma. In his *Animated Nature* he relates, with
faith and with perfect gravity, all the most absurd lies
which he could find in books of travels about gigantic
Patagonians, monkeys that preach sermons, nightingales
that repeat long conversations. " If he can tell a horse
from a cow," said Johnson, " that is the extent of his
knowledge of zoology." How little Goldsmith was
qualified to write about the physical sciences is sufficiently proved by two anecdotes. He on one occasion
denied that the sun is longer in the northern than in the
southern signs. It was in vain to cite the authority of

Maupertuis. " Maupertuis!" he cried; " I understand those matters better than Maupertuis." On another occasion he, in defiance of the evidence of his own senses, maintained obstinately, and even angrily, that he chewed his dinner by moving his upper jaw.

Yet, ignorant as Goldsmith was, few writers have done more to make the first steps in the laborious road to knowledge easy and pleasant. His compilations are widely distinguished from the compilations of ordinary bookmakers. He was a great, perhaps an unequalled, master of the arts of selection and condensation. In these respects his histories of Rome and of England, and still more his own abridgments of these histories, well deserve to be studied. In general nothing is less attractive than an epitome; but the epitomes of Goldsmith, even when most concise, are always amusing; and to read them is considered by intelligent children, not as a task, but as a pleasure.

Goldsmith might now be considered as a prosperous man. He had the means of living in comfort, and even in what to one who had so often slept in barns and on bulks must have been luxury. His fame was great and was constantly rising. He lived in what was intellectually far the best society of the kingdom, in a society in which no talent or accomplishment was wanting, and in which the art of conversation was cultivated with splendid success. There probably were never four talkers more admirable in four different ways than Johnson, Burke, Beauclerk, and Garrick; and Goldsmith was on terms of intimacy with all the four. He aspired to share in their colloquial renown; but never was ambition more unfortunate. It may seem strange that a man who wrote with so much perspicuity,

vivacity, and grace should have been, whenever he took
a part in conversation, an empty, noisy, blundering
rattle. But on this point the evidence is overwhelming.
So extraordinary was the contrast between Goldsmith's
published works and the silly things which he said, that
Horace Walpole described him as an inspired idiot.
" Noll," said Garrick, " wrote like an angel, and talked
like poor Poll." Chamier declared that it was a hard
exercise of faith to believe that so foolish a chatterer
could have really written the *Traveller*. Even Boswell could say, with contemptuous compassion, that
he liked very well to hear honest Goldsmith run on.
" Yes, sir," said Johnson; " but he should not like to
hear himself." Minds differ as rivers differ. There
are transparent and sparkling rivers from which it is
delightful to drink as they flow; to such rivers the
minds of such men as Burke and Johnson may be compared. But there are rivers of which the water when
first drawn is turbid and noisome, but becomes pellucid
as crystal, and delicious to the taste, if it be suffered to
stand till it has deposited a sediment; and such a river
is a type of the mind of Goldsmith. His first thoughts
on every subject were confused even to absurdity; but
they required only a little time to work themselves clear.
When he wrote they had that time; and therefore his
readers pronounced him a man of genius; but when he
talked he talked nonsense, and made himself the laughing-
stock of his hearers. He was painfully sensible of his
inferiority in conversation; he felt every failure keenly;
yet he had not sufficient judgment and self-command
to hold his tongue. His animal spirits and vanity were
always impelling him to try to do the one thing which he
could not do. After every attempt he felt he had exposed

himself, and writhed with shame and vexation; yet the
next moment he began again.

His associates seem to have regarded him with kindness, which, in spite of their admiration of his writings,
was not unmixed with contempt. In truth, there was
in his character much to love, but very little to respect.
His heart was soft, even to weakness: he was so generous
that he quite forgot to be just: he forgave injuries so
readily that he might be said to invite them: and was so
liberal to beggars that he had nothing left for his tailor
and his butcher. He was vain, sensual, frivolous, profuse,
improvident. One vice of a darker shade was imputed
to him, envy. But there is not the least reason to believe
that this bad passion, though it sometimes made him
wince and utter fretful exclamations, ever impelled him
to injure by wicked arts the reputation of any of his
rivals. The truth probably is, that he was not more
envious, but merely less prudent than his neighbours.
His heart was on his lips. All those small jealousies,
which are but too common among men of letters, but
which a man of letters who is also a man of the world
does his best to conceal, Goldsmith avowed with the
simplicity of a child. When he was envious instead
of affecting indifference, instead of damning with faint
praise, instead of doing injuries slily and in the dark,
he told everybody that he was envious. " Do not,
pray, do no talk of Johnson in such terms," he said
to Boswell; " you harrow up my very soul." George
Steevens and Cumberland were men far too cunning
to say such a thing. They would have echoed the
praises of the man they envied, and then have sent to
the newspapers anonymous libels upon him. Both
what was good and what was bad in Goldsmith's char-

acter was to his associates a perfect security that he
would never commit such villainy. He was neither
ill-natured enough, nor long-headed enough to be guilty
of any malicious act which required contrivance and
disguise.

Goldsmith has sometimes been represented as a man
of genius, cruelly treated by the world, and doomed
to struggle with difficulties which at last broke his heart.
But no representation can be more remote from the
truth. He did, indeed, go through much sharp misery
before he had done anything considerable in literature.
But, after his name had appeared on the title-page of
the *Traveller*, he had none to blame but himself for his
distresses. His average income during the last seven
years of his life certainly exceeded £400 a year; and
£400 a year ranked, among the incomes of that day, at
least as high as £800 a year would rank at present. A
single man living in the Temple with £400 a year might
then be called opulent. Not one in ten of the young
gentlemen of good families who were studying the law
there had so much. But all the wealth which Lord Clive
had brought from Bengal, and Sir Lawrence Dundas
from Germany, joined together would not have sufficed
for Goldsmith. He spent twice as much as he had. He
wore fine clothes, gave dinners of several courses, paid
court to venal beauties. He had also, it should be remembered, to the honour of his heart, though not of his
head, a guinea, or five, or ten, according to the state
of his purse, ready for any tale of distress, true or false.
But it was not in dress or feasting, in promiscuous amours
or promiscuous charities, that his chief expense lay. He
had been from boyhood a gambler, and at once the most
sanguine and the most unskilful of gamblers. For a time

he put off the day of inevitable ruin by temporary expedients. He obtained advances from booksellers, by promising to execute works which he never began. But at length this source of supply failed. He owed more than £2000; and he saw no hope of extrication from his embarrassments. His spirits and health gave way. He was attacked by a nervous fever, which he thought himself competent to treat. It would have been happy for him if his medical skill had been appreciated as justly by himself as by others. Notwithstanding the degree which he pretended to have received at Padua, he could procure no patients. "I do not practise," he once said, "I make it a rule to prescribe only for my friends." "Pray, dear Doctor," said Beauclerk, "alter your rule, and prescribe only for your enemies." Goldsmith now, in spite of this excellent advice, prescribed for himself. The remedy aggravated the malady. The sick man was induced to call in real physicians; and they at one time imagined that they had cured the disease. Still his weakness and restlessness continued. He could get no sleep, he could take no food. "You are worse," said one of his medical attendants, "than you should be from the degree of fever which you have. Is your mind at ease?" "No, it is not," were the last recorded words of Oliver Goldsmith. He died on the 3rd of April 1774, in his forty-sixth year. He was laid in the churchyard of the Temple; but the spot was not marked by any inscription, and is now forgotten. The coffin was followed by Burke and Reynolds. Both these great men were sincere mourners. Burke, when he heard of Goldsmith's death, had burst into a flood of tears. Reynolds had been so much moved by the news that he had flung aside his brush and palette for the day.

A short time after Goldsmith's death, a little poem appeared, which will, as long as our language lasts, associate the names of his two illustrious friends with his own. It has already been mentioned that he sometimes felt keenly the sarcasm which his wild blundering talk brought upon him. He was, not long before his last illness, provoked into retaliating. He wisely betook himself to his pen; and at that weapon he proved himself a match for all his assailants together. Within a small compass he drew with a singularly easy and vigorous pencil the characters of nine or ten of his intimate associates. Though this little work did not receive his last touches, it must always be regarded as a masterpiece. It is impossible, however, not to wish that four or five likenesses which have no interest for posterity were wanting to that noble gallery, and that their places were supplied by sketches of Johnson and Gibbon, as happy and vivid as the sketches of Burke and Garrick.

Some of Goldsmith's friends and admirers honoured him with a cenotaph in Westminster Abbey. Nollekens was the sculptor; and Johnson wrote the inscription. It is much to be lamented that Johnson did not leave to posterity a more durable and a more valuable memorial of his friend. A life of Goldsmith would have been an inestimable addition to the Lives of the Poets. No man appreciated Goldsmith's writings more justly than Johnson: no man was better acquainted with Goldsmith's character and habits: and no man was more competent to delineate with truth and spirit the peculiarities of a mind in which great powers were found in company with great weaknesses. But the list of poets to whose works Johnson was requested by the booksellers to furnish prefaces ended with Lyttleton, who died in 1773. The line seems to have been drawn expressly for the purpose of excluding the person whose portrait would have most fitly closed the series. Goldsmith, however, has been fortunate in his biographers. Within a few years his life has been written by Mr. Prior, by Mr. Washington Irving, and by Mr. Forster. The diligence of Mr. Prior deserves great praise; the style of Mr. Washington Irving is always pleasing; but the highest place must, in justice, be assigned to the eminently interesting work of Mr. Forster.

ROBERT LOUIS STEVENSON

(1850–1894)

Stevenson, the son of a Scottish engineer, was one of the greatest of story-tellers; but he was also a supremely great essayist. He was born near Edinburgh in 1850, and though he studied first for engineering and then for law, he had neither health nor enthusiasm enough for either of these. He became instead a story-teller, roaming the world in search of health and tales. He was a man of gentle character, who loved children and young people, and it was for them that his greatest work was done. The book from which these essays are taken, *Virginibus Puerisque*, was written in 1884 after a journey to America. It is a collection of admirable essays, dedicated, as the title suggests, to young people. Stevenson finally went to the South Seas in 1888 in a vain search for health, and died in Samoa in 1894. The essays are reprinted by permission of Mr. Lloyd Osbourne.

WALKING TOURS

It must not be imagined that a walking tour, as some would have us fancy, is merely a better or worse way of seeing the country. There are many ways of seeing landscape quite as good; and none more vivid, in spite of canting dilettantes, than from a railway train. But landscape on a walking tour is quite accessory. He who is indeed of the brotherhood does not voyage in quest of the picturesque but of certain jolly humours — of the hope and spirit with which the march begins at morning, and the peace and spiritual repletion of the evening's rest. He cannot tell whether he puts his knapsack on, or takes it off, with more delight. The excitement of the departure puts him in key for that of the arrival. Whatever he does is not only a reward in itself, but will be further rewarded in the sequel; and so pleasure leads on to pleasure in an endless chain. It is this that so few can understand; they will either be always lounging or always at five miles an hour; they do not play off the one against the other, prepare all day for the evening, and all evening for the next day. And, above all, it is here that your overwalker fails of comprehension. His heart rises against those who drink their curaçoa in liqueur glasses, when he himself can swill it in a brown John. He will not believe that the flavour is more delicate in the smaller dose. He will not believe that to walk this unconscionable distance is merely to stupefy and brutalize himself, and come to his inn, at night, with a sort of frost on his five wits, and a starless night of darkness in his spirit. Not for him the mild luminous evening of the temperate walker! He has nothing left of man but a physical need for bedtime and a double nightcap; and even his pipe, if he be a smoker, will be savourless and disenchanted. It is the fate of such an one to take twice as much trouble as is needed to obtain happiness, and miss the happiness in the end; he is the man of the proverb, in short, who goes farther and fares worse.

Now, to be properly enjoyed, a walking tour should be gone upon alone. If you go in a company, or even in pairs, it is no longer a walking tour in anything but name; it is something else and more in the nature of a picnic. A walking tour should be gone upon alone, because freedom is of the essence; because you should be able to stop and go on, and follow this way or that, as the freak takes you; and because you must have your own pace, and neither trot alongside a champion walker, nor mince in time with a girl. And then you must be open to all impressions and let your thoughts take colour from what you see. You should be as a pipe for any wind to play upon. " I cannot see the wit," says Hazlitt, " of walking and talking at the same time. When I am in the country, I wish to vegetate like the country," — which is the gist of all that can be said upon the matter. There should be no cackle of voices at your elbow, to jar on the meditative silence of the morning. And so long as a man is reasoning he cannot surrender himself to that fine intoxication that comes of much motion in the open air, that begins in a sort of dazzle and sluggishness of the brain, and ends in a peace that passes comprehension.

During the first day or so of any tour there are moments of bitterness, when the traveller feels more than coldly towards his knapsack, when he is half in a mind to throw it bodily over the hedge, and like Christian on a similar occasion, " give three leaps and go on singing ". And yet it soon acquires a property of easiness. It becomes magnetic; the spirit of the journey enters into it. And no sooner have you passed the straps over your shoulder than the lees of sleep are cleared from you, you pull yourself together with a shake, and fall at once into your stride. And surely, of all possible moods, this, in which a man takes the road, is the best. Of course, if he *will* keep thinking of his anxieties, if he *will* open the merchant Abudah's chest and walk arm-in-arm with the hag — why, wherever he is, and whether he walk fast or slow, the chances are that he will not be happy. And so much the more shame to himself! There are perhaps thirty men setting forth at that same hour, and I would lay a large wager there is not another dull face among the thirty. It would be a fine thing to follow, in a coat of darkness, one after another of these wayfarers, some summer morning, for the first few miles upon the road. This one, who walks fast, with a keen look in his eyes, is all concentrated in his own mind; he is up at his loom, weaving and weaving, to set the landscape to words. This one peers about, as he goes, among the grasses; he waits by the canal to watch the dragon-flies; he leans on the gate of the pasture, and cannot look enough upon the complacent kine. And here comes another, talking, laughing, and gesticulating to himself. His face changes from time to time, as indignation flashes from his eyes or anger clouds his forehead. He is composing articles, delivering orations, and conducting the most impassioned interviews by the way. A little farther on, and it is as like as not he will begin to sing. And well for him, supposing him to be no great master in that art, if he stumble across no stolid peasant at a corner; for on such an occasion, I scarcely know which is the more troubled, or whether it is worse to suffer the confusion of your troubadour, or the unfeigned alarm of your clown. A sedentary population, accustomed, besides, to the strange mechanical bearing of the common tramp, can in no wise explain to itself the gaiety of these passers-by. I knew one man who was arrested as a runaway lunatic, because, although a full-grown person with a red beard, he skipped as he went like a child. And you would be astonished if I were to tell you all the grave and learned heads who have confessed to me that, when on walking tours, they sang — and sang very ill — and had a pair of red ears when, as described above, the inauspicious peasant plumped into their arms from round a corner. And here, lest you should think I am exaggerating, is Hazlitt's own confession, from his essay *On Going a Journey*, which is so good that there should be a tax levied on all who have not read it: —

" Give me the clear blue sky over my head," says he, " and the green turf beneath my feet, a winding road before me, and a three hours' march to dinner — and then to thinking! It is hard if I cannot start some game on these lone heaths. I laugh, I run, I leap, I sing for joy."

Bravo! After that adventure of my friend with the policeman, you would not have cared, would you, to publish that in the first person? But we have no bravery nowadays, and, even in books, must all pretend to be as dull and foolish as our neighbours. It was not so with Hazlitt. And notice how learned he is (as, indeed, throughout the essay) in the theory of walking tours. He is none of your athletic men in purple stockings, who walk their fifty miles a day: three hours' march is his ideal. And then he must have a winding road, the epicure!

Yet there is one thing I object to in these words of his, one thing in the great master's practice that seems to me not wholly wise. I do not approve of that leaping and running. Both of these hurry the respiration; they both shake up the brain out of its glorious open-air confusion; and they both break the pace. Uneven walking is not so agreeable to the body, and it distracts and irritates the mind. Whereas, when once you have fallen into an equable stride, it requires no conscious thought from you to keep it up, and yet it prevents you from thinking earnestly of anything else. Like knitting, like the work of a copying clerk, it gradually neutralizes and sets to sleep the serious activity of the mind. We can think of this or that, lightly and laughingly, as a child thinks, or as we think in a morning doze; we can make puns or puzzle out acrostics, and trifle in a thousand ways with words and rhymes; but when it comes to honest work, when we come to gather ourselves together for an effort, we may sound the trumpet as loud and long as we please; the great barons of the mind will not rally to the standard, but sit, each one, at home, warming his hands over his own fire and brooding on his own private thought!

In the course of a day's walk, you see, there is much variance in the mood. From the exhilaration of the start, to the happy phlegm of the arrival, the change is certainly great. As the day goes on, the traveller moves from the one extreme towards the other. He becomes more and more incorporated with the material landscape, and the open-air drunkenness grows upon him with great strides, until he posts along the road, and sees everything about him, as in a cheerful dream. The first is certainly brighter, but the second stage is the more peaceful. A man does not make so many articles towards the end, nor does he laugh aloud; but the purely animal pleasures, the sense of physical well-being, the delight of every inhalation, of every time the muscles tighten down the thigh, console him for the absence of the others, and bring him to his destination still content.

Nor must I forget to say a word on bivouacs. You come to a milestone on a hill, or some place where deep ways meet under trees; and off goes the knapsack, and down you sit to smoke a pipe in the shade. You sink into yourself, and the birds come round and look at you; and your smoke dissipates upon the afternoon under the blue dome of heaven; and the sun lies warm upon your feet, and the cool air visits your neck and turns aside your open shirt. If you are not happy, you must have an evil conscience. You may dally as long as you like by the roadside. It is almost as if the millennium were arrived, when we shall throw our clocks and watches over the housetop, and remember time and seasons no more. Not to keep hours for a lifetime is, I was going to say, to live for ever. You have no idea, unless you have tried it, how endlessly long is a summer's day, that you measure out only by hunger, and bring to an end only when you are drowsy. I know a village where there are hardly any clocks, where no one knows more of the days of the week than by a sort of instinct for the fête on Sundays, and where only one person can tell you the day of the month, and she is generally wrong; and if people were aware how slow Time journeyed in that village, and what armfuls of spare hours he gives, over and above the bargain, to its wise inhabitants, I believe there would be a stampede out of London, Liverpool, Paris, and a variety of large towns, where the clocks lose their heads, and shake the hours out each one faster than the other, as though they were all in a wager. And all these foolish pilgrims would each bring his own misery along with him, in a watch-pocket! It is to be noticed, there were no clocks and watches in the much-vaunted days before the Flood. It follows, of course, there were no appointments, and punctuality was not yet thought upon. "Though ye take from a covetous man all his treasure," says Milton, "he has yet one jewel left; ye cannot deprive him of his covetousness." And so I would say of a modern man of business, you may do what you will for him, put him in Eden, give him the elixir of life — he has still a flaw at heart, he still has his business habits. Now, there is no time when business habits are more mitigated than on a walking tour. And so during these halts, as I say, you will feel almost free.

But it is at night, and after dinner, that the best hour comes. There are no such pipes to be smoked as those that follow a good day's march; the flavour of the tobacco is a thing to be remembered, it is so dry and aromatic, so full and so fine. If you wind up the evening with grog, you will own there was never such grog; at every sip a jocund tranquillity spreads about your limbs, and sits easily in your heart. If you read a book — and you will never do so save by fits and starts — you find the language strangely racy and harmonious; words take a new meaning; single sentences possess the ear for half an hour together; and the writer endears himself to you, at every page, by the nicest coincidence of sentiment. It seems as if it were a book you had written yourself in a dream. To all we have read on such occasions we look back with special favour. " It was on the 10th of April, 1798," says Hazlitt, with amorous precision, " that I sat down to a volume of the new *Héloïse*, at the Inn at Llangollen, over a bottle of sherry and a cold chicken." I should wish to quote more, for though we are mighty fine fellows nowadays, we cannot write like Hazlitt. And, talking of that, a volume of Hazlitt's essays would be a capital pocket-book on such a journey; so would a volume of Heine's songs; and for *Tristram Shandy* I can pledge a fair experience.

If the evening be fine and warm, there is nothing better in life than to lounge before the inn door in the

sunset, or lean over the parapet of the bridge, to watch
the weeds and the quick fishes. It is then, if ever, that
you taste Joviality to the full significance of that audacious
word. Your muscles are so agreeably slack, you feel so
clean and so strong and so idle, that whether you move
or sit still, whatever you do is done with pride and a
kingly sort of pleasure. You fall in talk with any one,
wise or foolish, drunk or sober. And it seems as if a hot
walk purged you, more than of anything else, of all
narrowness and pride, and left curiosity to play its part
freely, as in a child or a man of science. You lay aside
all your own hobbies, to watch provincial humours de-
velop themselves before you, now as a laughable farce,
and now grave and beautiful like an old tale.

Or perhaps you are left to your own company for the
night, and surly weather imprisons you by the fire.
You may remember how Burns, numbering past pleasures,
dwells upon the hours when he has been " happy thinking ". It is a phrase that may well perplex a poor modern,
girt about on every side by clocks and chimes, and
haunted, even at night, by flaming dial-plates. For we
were all so busy, and have so many far-off projects to
realize, and castles in the fire to turn into solid habitable
mansions on a gravel soil, that we can find no time for
pleasure trips into the Land of Thought and among the
Hills of Vanity. Changed times, indeed, when we must
sit all night, beside the fire, with folded hands; and a
changed world for most of us, when we find we can pass
the hours without discontent, and be happy thinking.
We are in such haste to be doing, to be writing, to be
gathering gear, to make our voice audible a moment in
the derisive silence of eternity, that we forget that one
thing, of which these are but the parts — namely, to

live. We fall in love, we drink hard, we run to and fro upon the earth like frightened sheep. And now you are to ask yourself if, when all is done, you would not have been better to sit by the fire at home and be happy thinking. To sit still and contemplate — to remember the faces of women without desire, to be pleased by the great deeds of men without envy, to be everything and everywhere in sympathy, and yet content to remain where and what you are — is not this to know both wisdom and virtue, and to dwell with happiness? After all, it is not they who carry flags, but they who look upon it from a private chamber, who have the fun of the procession. And once you are at that, you are in the very humour of all social heresy. It is no time for shuffling, or for big, empty words. If you ask yourself what you mean by fame, riches, or learning, the answer is far to seek; and you go back into that kingdom of light imaginations, which seem so vain in the eyes of Philistines perspiring after wealth, and so momentous to those who are stricken with the disproportions of the world, and, in the face of the gigantic stars, cannot stop to split differences between two degrees of the infinitesimally small, such as a tobacco-pipe or the Roman Empire, a million of money or a fiddlestick's end.

You lean from the window, your last pipe reeking whitely into the darkness, your body full of delicious pains, your mind enthroned in the seventh circle of content; when suddenly the moon changes, the weather-cock goes about, and you ask yourself one question more: whether, for the interval, you have been the wisest philosopher or the most egregious of donkeys? Human experience is not yet able to reply; but at least you have had a fine moment, and looked down upon all the kingdoms of the earth. And whether it was wise or foolish, to-morrow's travel will carry you, body and mind, into some different parish of the infinite.

A PLEA FOR GAS LAMPS

Cities given, the problem was to light them. How to conduct individual citizens about the burgess-warren, when once heaven had withdrawn its leading luminary? or — since we live in a scientific age — when once our spinning planet has turned its back upon the sun? The moon, from time to time, was doubtless very helpful; the stars had a cheery look among the chimney-pots; and a cresset here and there, on church or citadel, produced a fine pictorial effect, and, in places where the ground lay unevenly, held out the right hand of conduct to the benighted. But sun, moon, and stars abstracted or concealed, the night-faring inhabitant had to fall back — we speak on the authority of old prints — upon stable lanthorns two stories in height. Many holes, drilled in the conical turret-roof of this vagabond Pharos, let up spouts of dazzlement into the bearer's eyes; and as he paced forth in the ghostly darkness, carrying his own sun by a ring about his finger, day and night swung to and fro and up and down about his footsteps. Blackness haunted his path; he was beleaguered by goblins as he went; and, curfew being struck, he found no light but that he travelled in throughout the township.

Closely following on this epoch of migratory lanthorns in a world of extinction, came the era of oil-lights, hard to kindle, easy to extinguish, pale and wavering in the hour of their endurance. Rudely puffed the winds of heaven; roguishly clomb up the all-destructive urchin; and, lo! in a moment night re-established her void empire, and the cit groped along the wall, suppered but bedless, occult from guidance, and sorrily wading in the kennels. As if gamesome winds and gamesome youths were not sufficient, it was the habit to sling these fable luminaries from house to house above the fairway. There, on invisible cordage, let them swing! And suppose some crane-necked general to go speeding by on a tall charger, spurring the destiny of nations, red-hot in expedition, there would indubitably be some effusion of military blood, and oaths, and a certain crash of glass; and while the chieftain rode forward with a purple coxcomb, the street would be left to original darkness, unpiloted, unvoyageable, a province of the desert night.

The conservative, looking before and after, draws from each contemplation the matter for content. Out of the age of gas lamps he glances back slightingly at the mirk and glimmer in which his ancestors wandered; his heart waxes jocund at the contrast; nor do his lips refrain from a stave, in the highest style of poetry, lauding progress and the golden mean. When gas first spread along a city, mapping it forth about evenfall for the eye of observant birds, a new age had begun for sociality and corporate pleasure-seeking, and begun with proper circumstance, becoming its own birthright. The work of Prometheus had advanced by another stride. Mankind and its supper parties were no longer at the mercy of a few miles of sea-fog; sundown no longer emptied the promenade; and the day was lengthened out to every man's fancy. The city-folk had stars of their own; biddable domesticated stars.

It is true that these were not so steady, nor yet so clear, as their originals; nor indeed was their lustre so elegant as that of the best wax candles. But then the gas stars, being nearer at hand, were more practically efficacious than Jupiter himself. It is true, again, that they did not unfold their rays with the appropriate spontaneity of the planets, coming out along the firmament one after another, as the need arises. But the lamplighters took to their heels every evening, and ran with a good heart. It was pretty to see man thus emulating the punctuality of heaven's orbs; and though perfection was not absolutely reached, and now and then an individual may have been knocked on the head by the ladder of the flying functionary, yet people commended his zeal in a proverb, and taught their children to say, " God bless the lamplighter!" And since his passage was a piece of the day's programme, the children were well pleased to repeat the benediction, not, of course, in so many words, which would have been improper, but in some chaste circumlocution, suitable for infant lips.

God bless him, indeed! For the term of his twilight diligence is near at hand; and for not much longer shall we watch him speeding up the street, and, at measured intervals, knocking another luminous hole into the dusk. The Greeks would have made a noble myth of such an one; how he distributed starlight, and, as soon as the need was over, re-collected it; and the little bull's-eye, which was his instrument, and held enough fire to kindle a whole parish, would have been fitly commemorated in the legend. Now, like all heroic tasks, his labours draw towards apotheosis, and in the light of victory himself shall disappear. For another advance has been effected. Our tame stars are to come out in future, not one by one, but all in a body and at once. A sedate electrician somewhere in a back office touches a spring — and behold! from one end to another of the city, from east to west, from the Alexandra to the Crystal Palace, there is light! *Fiat Lux*, says the sedate electrician. What a spectacle, on some clear, dark nightfall, from the edge of Hampstead Hill, when in a moment, in the twinkling of an eye, the design of the monstrous city flashes into vision — a glittering hieroglyph many square miles in extent; and when, to borrow and debase an image, all the evening street lamps burst together into song! Such is the spectacle of the future, preluded the other day by the experiment in Pall Mall. Star-rise by electricity, the most romantic flight of civilization; the compensatory benefit for an innumerable array of factories and bankers' clerks. To the artistic spirit exercised about Thirlmere, here is a crumb of consolation; consolatory, at least, to such of them as look out upon the world through seeing eyes, and contentedly accept beauty where it comes.

But the conservative, while lauding progress, is ever timid of innovation; his is the hand upheld to counsel pause; his is the signal advising slow advance. The word *electricity* now sounds the note of danger. In Paris, at the mouth of the Passage des Princes, in the place before the Opera portico, and in the Rue Drouot at the *Figaro* office, a new sort of urban star now shines out nightly, horrible, unearthly, obnoxious to the human eye; a lamp for a nightmare! Such a light as this should shine only on murders and public crime, or along the corridors of lunatic asylums, a horror to heighten horror. To look at it only once is to fall in love with gas, which

gives a warm domestic radiance fit to eat by. Mankind,
you would have thought, might have remained content
with what Prometheus stole for them and not gone
fishing the profound heaven with kites to catch and
domesticate the wildfire of the storm. Yet here we have
the levin brand at our doors, and it is proposed that we
should henceforward take our walks abroad in the glare
of permanent lightning. A man need not be very superstitious if he scruple to follow his pleasures by the light
of the Terror that Flieth, nor very epicurean if he prefer
to see the face of beauty more becomingly displayed.
That ugly blinding glare may not improperly advertise
the home of slanderous *Figaro*, which is a back-shop to
the infernal regions; but where soft joys prevail, where
people are convoked to pleasure and the philosopher
looks on smiling and silent, where love and laughter and
deifying wine abound, there, at least, let the old mild
lustre shine upon the ways of man.

CHILD'S PLAY

The regret we have for our childhood is not wholly
justifiable: so much a man may lay down without fear
of public ribaldry; for although we shake our heads
over the change, we are not unconscious of the manifold
advantages of our new state. What we lose in generous
impulse, we more than gain in the habit of generously
watching others; and the capacity to enjoy Shakespeare
may balance a lost aptitude for playing at soldiers.
Terror is gone out of our lives, moreover; we no longer
see the devil in the bed-curtains nor lie awake to listen

to the wind. We go to school no more; and if we have only exchanged one drudgery for another (which is by no means sure), we are set free for ever from the daily fear of chastisement. And yet a great change has overtaken us; and although we do not enjoy ourselves less, at least we take our pleasure differently. We need pickles nowadays to make Wednesday's cold mutton please our Friday's appetite; and I can remember the time when to call it red venison, and tell myself a hunter's story, would have made it more palatable than the best of sauces. To the grown person, cold mutton is cold mutton all the world over; not all the mythology ever invented by man will make it better or worse to him; the broad fact, the clamant reality, of the mutton carries away before it such seductive figments. But for the child it is still possible to weave an enchantment over eatables; and if he has but read of a dish in a story-book, it will be heavenly manna to him for a week.

If a grown man does not like eating and drinking and exercise, if he is not something positive in his tastes, it means he has a feeble body and should have some medicine; but children may be pure spirits, if they will, and take their enjoyment in a world of moonshine. Sensation does not count for so much in our first years as afterwards; something of the swaddling numbness of infancy clings about us; we see and touch and hear through a sort of golden mist. Children, for instance, are able enough to see, but they have no great faculty for looking; they do not use their eyes for the pleasure of using them, but for by-ends of their own; and the things I call to mind seeing most vividly, were not beautiful in themselves, but merely interesting or enviable to me as I thought they might be turned to practical account in play. Nor is the sense of touch so clean and poignant in children as it is in a man. If you will turn over your old memories, I think the sensations of this sort you remember will be somewhat vague, and come to not much more than a blunt, general sense of heat on summer days, or a blunt, general sense of well-being in bed. And here, of course, you will understand pleasurable sensations; for overmastering pain — the most deadly and tragical element in life, and the true commander of man's soul and body — alas! pain has its own way with all of us; it breaks in, a rude visitant, upon the fairy garden where the child wanders in a dream, no less surely than it rules upon the field of battle, or sends the immortal war-god whimpering to his father; and innocence, no more than philosophy, can protect us from this sting. As for taste, when we bear in mind the excesses of unmitigated sugar which delight a youthful palate, " it is surely no very cynical asperity " to think taste a character of the maturer growth. Smell and hearing are perhaps more developed; I remember many scents, many voices, and a great deal of spring singing in the woods. But hearing is capable of vast improvement as a means of pleasure; and there is all the world between gaping wonderment at the jargon of birds, and the emotion with which a man listens to articulate music.

At the same time, and step by step with this increase in the definition and intensity of what we feel which accompanies our growing age, another change takes place in the sphere of intellect, by which all things are transformed and seen through theories and associations as through coloured windows. We make to ourselves day by day, out of history, and gossip, and economical speculations, and God knows what, a medium in which we walk and through which we look abroad. We study shop windows with other eyes than in our childhood, never to wonder, not always to admire, but to make and modify our little incongruous theories about life. It is no longer the uniform of a soldier that arrests our attention; but perhaps the flowing carriage of a woman, or perhaps a countenance that has been vividly stamped with passion and carries an adventurous story written in its lines. The pleasure of surprise is passed away; sugar-loaves and water-carts seem mighty tame to encounter; and we walk the streets to make romances and to sociologize. Nor must we deny that a good many of us walk them solely for the purposes of transit or in the interest of a livelier digestion. These, indeed, may look back with mingled thoughts upon their childhood, but the rest are in a better case; they know more than when they were children, they understand better, their desires and sympathies answer more nimbly to the provocation of the senses, and their minds are brimming with interest as they go about the world.

According to my contention, this is a flight to which children cannot rise. They are wheeled in perambulators or dragged about by nurses in a pleasing stupor. A vague, faint, abiding wonderment possesses them. Here and there some specially remarkable circumstance, such as a water-cart or a guardsman, fairly penetrates into the seat of thought and calls them, for half a moment, out of themselves; and you may see them, still towed forward sideways by the inexorable nurse as by a sort of destiny, but still staring at the bright object in their wake. It may be some minutes before another such moving spectacle reawakens them to the world in which they dwell. For other children, they almost invariably show some intelligent sympathy. " There is a fine fellow making mud pies," they seem to say; " that I can understand: there is some sense in mud pies." But the doings of their elders, unless where they are speakingly picturesque or recommend themselves by the quality of being easily imitable, they let them go over their heads (as we say) without the least regard. If it were not for this perpetual imitation, we should be tempted to fancy they despised us outright, or only considered us in the light of creatures brutally strong and brutally silly: among whom they condescended to dwell in obedience like a philosopher at a barbarous court. At times, indeed, they display an arrogance of disregard that is truly staggering. Once, when I was groaning aloud with physical pain, a young gentleman came into the room and nonchalantly inquired if I had seen his bow and arrow. He made no account of my groans, which he accepted, as he had to accept so much else, as a piece of the inexplicable conduct of his elders; and like a wise young gentleman, he would waste no wonder on the subject. Those elders, who care so little for rational enjoyment, and are even the enemies of rational enjoyment for others, he had accepted without understanding and without complaint, as the rest of us accept the scheme of the universe.

We grown people can tell ourselves a story, give and take strokes until the bucklers ring, ride far and fast, marry, fall, and die; all the while sitting quietly by the fire or lying prone in bed. This is exactly what a child cannot do, or does not do, at least, when he can find anything else. He works all with lay figures and stage properties. When his story comes to the fighting, he must rise, get something by way of a sword and have a set-to with a piece of furniture, until he is out of breath. When he comes to ride with the king's pardon, he must bestride a chair, which he will so hurry and belabour and on which he will so furiously demean himself, that the messenger will arrive, if not bloody with spurring, at least fiery red with haste. If his romance involves an accident upon a cliff, he must clamber in person about the chest of drawers and fall bodily upon the carpet, before his imagination is satisfied. Lead soldiers, dolls, all toys, in short, are in the same category and answer the same end. Nothing can stagger a child's faith; he accepts the clumsiest substitutes and can swallow the most staring incongruities. The chair he has just been besieging as a castle, or valiantly cutting to the ground as a dragon, is taken away for the accommodation of a morning visitor, and he is nothing abashed; he can skirmish by the hour with a stationary coal-scuttle; in the midst of the enchanted pleasance he can see, without sensible shock, the gardener soberly digging potatoes for the day's dinner. He can make abstraction of whatever does not fit into his fable; and he puts his eyes into his pocket, just as we hold our noses in an unsavoury lane. And so it is, that although the ways of children cross with those of their elders in a hundred places daily, they never go in the same direction nor so much as lie in the same element. So may the telegraph wires inter-sect the line of the high road, or so might a landscape painter and a bagman visit the same country, and yet move in different worlds.

People struck with these spectacles cry aloud about the power of imagination in the young. Indeed there may be two words to that. It is, in some ways, but a pedestrian fancy that the child exhibits. It is the grown people who make the nursery stories; all the children do, is jealously to preserve the text. One out of a dozen reasons why *Robinson Crusoe* should be so popular with youth, is that it hits their level in this matter to a nicety; Crusoe was always at makeshifts and had, in so many words, to *play* at a great variety of professions; and then the book is all about tools, and there is nothing that delights a child so much. Hammers and saw belong to a province of life that positively calls for imitation. The juvenile lyrical drama, of the most ancient Thespian model, wherein the trades of mankind are successively simulated to the running burthen " On a cold and frosty morning ", gives a good instance of the artistic taste in children. And this need for overt action and lay figures testifies to a defect in the child's imagination which prevents him from carrying out his novels in the privacy of his own heart. He does not yet know enough of the world and men. His experience is incomplete. That stage-wardrobe and scene-room that we call the memory is so ill-provided, that he can overtake few combinations and body out few stories, to his own content, without some external aid. He is at the experimental stage; he is not sure how one would feel in certain circumstances; to make sure, he must come as near trying it as his means permit. And so here is young heroism with a wooden sword, and mothers practise their kind vocation over a bit of jointed stick. It may be laughable enough just now; but it is these same people and these same thoughts, that not long hence, when they are on the theatre of life, will make you weep and tremble. For children think very much the same thoughts and dream the same dreams as bearded men and marriageable women. No

one is more romantic. Fame and honour, the love of
young men and the love of mothers, the business man's
pleasure in method, all these and others they anticipate
and rehearse in their play hours. Upon us, who are
further advanced and fairly dealing with the threads of
destiny, they only glance from time to time to glean a
hint for their own mimetic reproduction. Two children
playing at soldiers are far more interesting to each other
than one of the scarlet beings whom both are busy
imitating. This is perhaps the greatest oddity of all.
" Art for art " is their motto; and the doings of grown
folk are only interesting as the raw material for play.
Not Théophile Gautier, not Flaubert, can look more
callously upon life, or rate the reproduction more highly
over the reality; and they will parody an execution, a
deathbed, or the funeral of the young man of Nain, with
all the cheerfulness in the world.

The true parallel for play is not to be found, of course,
in conscious art, which, though it be derived from play,
is itself an abstract, impersonal thing, and depends
largely upon philosophical interests beyond the scope of
childhood. It is when we make castles in the air and
personate the leading character in our own romances,
that we return to the spirit of our first years. Only,
there are several reasons why the spirit is no longer so
agreeable to indulge. Nowadays, when we admit this
personal element into our divagations we are apt to stir
up uncomfortable and sorrowful memories, and remind
ourselves sharply of old wounds. Our day-dreams can
no longer lie all in the air like a story in the *Arabian
Nights*; they read to us rather like the history of a period
in which we ourselves had taken part, where we come
across many unfortunate passages, and find our own

conduct smartly reprimanded. And then the child, mind you, acts his parts. He does not merely repeat them to himself; he leaps, he runs, and sets the blood agog over all his body. And so his play breathes him; and he no sooner assumes a passion than he gives it vent. Alas! when we betake ourselves to our intellectual form of play, sitting quietly by the fire or lying prone in bed, we rouse many hot feelings for which we can find no outlet. Substitutes are not acceptable to the mature mind, which desires the thing itself; and even to rehearse a triumphant dialogue with one's enemy, although it is perhaps the most satisfactory piece of play still left within our reach, is not entirely satisfying, and is even apt to lead to a visit and an interview which may be the reverse of triumphant after all.

In the child's world of dim sensation, play is all in all. " Making believe " is the gist of his whole life, and he cannot so much as take a walk except in character. I could not learn my alphabet without some suitable *mise-en-scène*, and had to act a business man in an office before I could sit down to my book. Will you kindly question your memory, and find out how much you did, work or pleasure, in good faith and soberness, and for how much you had to cheat yourself with some invention? I remember, as though it were yesterday, the expansion of spirit, the dignity and self-reliance, that came with a pair of mustachios in burnt cork, even when there was none to see. Children are even content to forgo what we call the realities, and prefer the shadow to the substance. When they might be speaking intelligibly together, they chatter senseless gibberish by the hour, and are quite happy because they are making believe to speak French. I have said already how even the imperious appetite of hunger suffers itself to be gulled and led by the nose with the fag end of an old song. And it goes deeper than this: when children are together even a meal is felt as an interruption in the business of life; and they must find some imaginative sanction, and tell themselves some sort of story, to account for, to colour, to render entertaining, the simple processes of eating and drinking. What wonderful fancies I have heard evolved out of the pattern upon tea-cups! — from which there followed a code of rules and a whole world of excitement, until tea-drinking began to take rank as a game. When my cousin and I took our porridge of a morning, we had a device to enliven the course of the meal. He ate his with sugar, and explained it to be a country continually buried under snow. I took mine with milk, and explained it to be a country suffering gradual inundation. You can imagine us exchanging bulletins; how here was an island still unsubmerged, here a valley not yet covered with snow; what inventions were made; how his population lived in cabins on perches and travelled on stilts, and how mine was always in boats; how the interest grew furious, as the last corner of safe ground was cut off on all sides and grew smaller every moment; and how, in fine, the food was of altogether secondary importance, and might even have been nauseous, so long as we seasoned it with these dreams. But perhaps the most exciting moments I ever had over a meal, were in the case of calves'-feet jelly. It was hardly possible not to believe — and you may be sure, so far from trying, I did all I could to favour the illusion — that some part of it was hollow, and that sooner or later my spoon would lay open the secret tabernacle of the golden rock.

There, might some miniature *Red Beard* await his hour; there, might one find the treasures of the *Forty Thieves*, and bewildered Cassim beating about the walls. And so I quarried on slowly, with bated breath, savouring the interest. Believe me, I had little palate left for the jelly; and though I preferred the taste when I took cream with it, I used often to go without, because the cream dimmed the transparent fractures.

Even with games, this spirit is authoritative with right-minded children. It is thus that hide-and-seek has so pre-eminent a sovereignty, for it is the well-spring of romance, and the actions and the excitement to which it gives rise lend themselves to almost any sort of fable. And thus cricket, which is a mere matter of dexterity, palpably about nothing and for no end, often fails to satisfy infantile craving. It is a game, if you like, but not a game of play. You cannot tell yourself a story about cricket; and the activity it calls forth can be justified on no rational theory. Even football, although it admirably simulates the tug and the ebb and flow of battle, has presented difficulties to the mind of young sticklers after verisimilitude; and I knew at least one little boy who was mightily exercised about the presence of the ball, and had to spirit himself up, whenever he came to play, with an elaborate story of enchantment, and take the missile as a sort of talisman bandied about in conflict between two Arabian nations.

To think of such a frame of mind is to become disquieted about the bringing up of children. Surely they dwell in a mythological epoch, and are not the contemporaries of their parents. What can they think of them? what can they make of these bearded or petticoated giants who look down upon their games? who move upon a cloudy Olympus, following unknown designs apart from rational enjoyment? who profess the tenderest solicitude for children, and yet every now and again reach down out of their altitude and terribly vindicate the prerogatives of age? Off goes the child, corporally smarting, but morally rebellious. Were there ever such unthinkable deities as parents? I would give a great deal to know what, in nine cases out of ten, is the child's unvarnished feeling. A sense of past cajolery; a sense of personal attraction, at best very feeble; above all, I should imagine, a sense of terror for the untried residue of mankind: go to make up the attraction that he feels. No wonder, poor little heart, with such a weltering world in front of him, if he clings to the hand he knows! The dread irrationality of the whole affair, as it seems to children, is a thing we are all too ready to forget. " Oh, why," I remember passionately wondering, " why can we not all be happy and devote ourselves to play?" And when children do philosophize, I believe it is usually to very much the same purpose.

One thing, at least, comes very clearly out of these considerations: that whatever we are to expect at the hands of children, it should not be any peddling exactitude about matters of fact. They walk in a vain show, and among mists and rainbows; they are passionate after dreams and unconcerned about realities; speech is a difficult art not wholly learned; and there is nothing in their own tastes or purposes to teach them what we mean by abstract truthfulness. When a bad writer is inexact, even if he can look back on half a century of years, we charge him with incompetence and not with dishonesty. And why not extend the same allowance to imperfect speakers? Let a stockbroker be dead stupid about poetry, or a poet inexact in the details of business, and we excuse them heartily from blame. But show us a miserable, unbreeched, human entity, whose whole profession it is to take a tub for a fortified town and a shaving-brush for the deadly stiletto, and who passes three-fourths of his time in a dream and the rest in open self-deception, and we expect him to be as nice upon a matter of fact as a scientific expert bearing evidence. Upon my heart, I think it less than decent. You do not consider how little the child sees, or how swift he is to weave what he has seen into bewildering fiction; and that he cares no more for what you call truth, than you for a gingerbread dragoon.

I am reminded, as I write, that the child is very inquiring as to the precise truth of stories. But indeed this is a very different matter, and one bound up with the subject of play, and the precise amount of playfulness, or playability, to be looked for in the world. Many such burning questions must arise in the course of nursery education. Among the fauna of this planet, which already embraces the pretty soldier and the terrifying Irish beggar-man, is, or is not, the child to expect a Bluebeard or a Cormoran? Is he, or is he not, to look out for magicians, kindly and potent? May he, or may he not, reasonably hope to be cast away upon a desert island, or turned to such diminutive proportions that he can live on equal terms with his lead soldiery, and go a cruise in his own toy schooner? Surely all these are practical questions to a neophyte entering upon life with a view to play. Precision upon such a point, the child can understand. But if you merely ask him of his past behaviour, as to who threw such a stone, for instance, or struck such and such a match; or whether he

had looked into a parcel or gone by a forbidden path —
why, he can see no moment in the inquiry, and it is ten
to one he has already half-forgotten and half-bemused
himself with subsequent imaginings.

It would be easy to leave them in their native cloud-
land, where they figure so prettily — pretty like flowers
and innocent like dogs. They will come out of their
gardens soon enough, and have to go into offices and the
witness-box. Spare them yet a while, O conscientious
parent! Let them doze among their playthings yet a
little! for who knows what a rough, warfaring existence
lies before them in the future?

AUGUSTINE BIRRELL

(1850–1933)

During his long life, Augustine Birrell distinguished himself in several spheres — as a politician, as a writer, and as a lawyer. He was a man of wide scholarship and deep insight, and a noted literary critic. His essays are marked by this scholarship, and by his kindly humour.

OLD BOOKSELLERS

There has just been a small flutter amongst those who used to be called stationers or text-writers in the good old days, before printing was, and when even Peers of the Realm (now so highly educated) could not sign their names, or, at all events, preferred not to do so — booksellers they are now styled — and the question which agitates them is discount. Having mentioned this, one naturally passes on.

No great trade has an obscurer history than the book trade. It seems to lie choked in mountains of dust which it would be suicidal to disturb. Men have lived from time to time of literary skill — Dr. Johnson was one of them — who had knowledge, extensive and peculiar, of the traditions and practices of " the trade ", as it is proudly styled by its votaries; but nobody has ever thought it worth his while to make record of his knowledge, which accordingly perished with him, and is now irrecoverably lost.

In old days booksellers were also publishers, frequently printers, and sometimes paper-makers. Jacob Tonson not only owned Milton's *Paradise Lost* — for all time, as he fondly thought, for little did he dream of the fierce construction the House of Lords was to put upon the Copyright Act of Queen Anne — not only was Dryden's publisher, but also kept shop in Chancery Lane, and sold books across the counter. He allowed no discount, but, so we are told, " spoke his mind upon all occasions, and flattered no one ", not even glorious John.

For a long time past the trades of bookselling and book-publishing have been carried on apart. This has doubtless rid booksellers of all the unpopularity which formerly belonged to them in their other capacity. This unpopularity is now heaped as a whole upon the publishers, who certainly need not dread the doom awaiting those of whom the world speaks well.

A tendency of the two trades to grow together again is perhaps noticeable. For my part, I wish they would. Some publishers are already booksellers, but the books they sell are usually only new books. Now it is obvious that the true bookseller sells books both old and new. Some booksellers are occasional publishers. May each usurp — or, rather, reassume — the business of the other, whilst retaining his own!

The world, it must be admitted, owes a great deal of whatever information it possesses about the professions, trades, and occupations practised and carried on in its midst to those who have failed in them. Prosperous men talk " shop ", but seldom write it. The book that tells us most about booksellers and bookselling in bygone days is the work of a crack-brained fellow who pub-

lished and sold in the reigns of Queen Anne and George
I, and died in 1733 in great poverty and obscurity. I
refer to John Dunton, whose *Life and Errors* in the
edition in two volumes edited by J. B. Nichols, and
published in 1818, is a common book enough in the
second-hand shops, and one which may be safely recommended to everyone, except, indeed, to the unfortunate man or woman who is not an adept in the art,
craft, or mystery of skipping.

The book will strangely remind the reader of Amory's
Life of John Buncle — those queer volumes to which
many a reader has been sent by Hazlitt's intoxicating
description of them in his *Round Table*, and a few perhaps by a shy allusion contained in one of the essays of
Elia. The real John Dunton has not the boundless
spirits of the fictitious John Buncle; but in their religious fervour, their passion for flirtation, their tireless
egotism, and their love of character-sketching, they
greatly resemble one another.

It is this last characteristic that imparts real value to
Dunton's book, and makes it, despite its verbiage and
tortuosity, throb with human interest. For example,
he gives us a short sketch of no less than 135 then living
London booksellers in this style: " Mr. Newton is full
of kindness and good-nature. He is affable and cour-
teous in trade, and is none of those men of forty whose
religion is yet to chuse, for his mind (like his looks) is
serious and grave; and his neighbours tell me his understanding does not improve too fast for his practice, for
he is not religious by start or sally, but is well fixed in
the faith and practice of a Church of England man —
and has a handsome wife into the bargain."

Most of the 135 booksellers were good men, according to Dunton, but not all. " Mr. Lee in Lombard Street. Such a pirate, such a cormorant was never before. Copies, books, men, shops, all was one. He held no propriety right or wrong, good or bad, till at last he began to be known; and the booksellers, not enduring so ill a man among them, spewed him out, and off he marched to Ireland, where he acted as *felonious Lee* as he did in London. And as Lee lived a thief, so he died a hypocrite; for being asked on his death-bed if he would forgive Mr. C. (that had formerly wronged him), ' Yes,' said Lee, ' if I die, I forgive him; but if I happen to live, I am resolved to be revenged on him.' "

The Act of Union destroyed the trade of these pirates, but their felonious editions of eighteenth-century authors still abound. Mr. Gladstone, I need scarcely say, was careful in his Home Rule Bill (which was denounced by thousands who never read a line of it) to withdraw copyright from the scope of action of his proposed Dublin Parliament.

There are nearly eleven hundred brief character-sketches in Dunton's book, of all sorts and kinds, but with a preference for bookish people, divines, both of the Establishment and out of it, printers and authors. Sometimes, indeed, the description is short enough, and tells one very little. To many readers, references so curt to people of whom they never heard, and whose names are recorded nowhere else, save on their mouldering grave-stones, may seem tedious and trivial, but for others they will have a strange fascination. Here are a few examples:

" Affable *Wiggins*. His conversation is general but never impertinent.

" The kind and golden *Venables*. He is so good a

man, and so truly charitable, he that will write of him must still write more.

"Mr. *Bury* — my old neighbour in Redcross Street. He is a plain honest man, sells the best coffee in all the neighbourhood, and lives in this world like a spiritual stranger and pilgrim in a foreign country.

"Anabaptist (alias *Elephant*) *Smith*. He was a man of great sincerity and happy contentment in all circumstances of life."

If an affection for passages of this kind be condemned as trivial, and akin to the sentimentalism of the man in Calverley's poem who wept over a box labelled "This side up", I will shelter myself behind Carlyle, who was evidently deeply moved, as his review of Boswell's Johnson proves, by the life-history of Mr. F. Lewis, "of whose birth, death, and whole terrestrial *res gestae* this only, and, strange enough, this actually, survives — 'Sir, he lived in London, and hung loose upon society. *Stat* PARVI *hominis umbra*.'" On that peg Carlyle's imagination hung a whole biography.

Dunton, who was the son of the Rector of Aston Clinton, was apprenticed, about 1675, to a London bookseller. He had from the beginning a great turn both for religion and love. He, to use his own phrase, "sat under the powerful ministry of Mr. Doolittle". "One Lord's day, and I remember it with sorrow, I was to hear the Rev. Mr. Doolittle, and it was then and there the beautiful Rachel Seaton gave me that fatal wound."

The first book Dunton ever printed was by the Rev. Mr. Doolittle, and was of an eminently religious character.

"One Lord's Day (and I am very sensible of the sin)

I was strolling about just as my fancy led me, and, stepping into Dr. Annesley's meeting-place — where, instead of engaging my attention to what the Doctor said, I suffered both my mind and eyes to run at random — I soon singled out a young lady that almost charmed me dead; but, having made my inquiries, I found to my sorrow she was pre-engaged." However, Dunton was content with the elder sister, one of the three daughters of Dr. Annesley. The one he first saw became the wife of the Reverend Samuel Wesley, and the mother of John and Charles. The third daughter is said to have been married to Daniel De Foe.

As soon as he was out of his apprenticeship, Dunton set up business as a publisher and bookseller. He says grimly enough:

" A man should be well furnished with an honest policy if he intends to set out to the world nowadays. And this is no less necessary in a bookseller than in any other tradesman, for in that way there are plots and counter-plots, and a whole army of hackney authors that keep their grinders moving by the travail of their pens. These gormandisers will eat you the very life out of a *copy* so soon as ever it appears, for as the times go, *Original* and *Abridgement* are almost reckoned as necessary as man and wife."

The mischief to which Dunton refers was permitted by the stupidity of the judges, who refused to consider an abridgment of a book any interference with its copyright. Some learned judges have, indeed, held that an abridger is a benefactor, but as his benefactions are not his own, but another's, a shorter name might be found for him. The law on the subject is still uncertain.

Dunton proceeds: " Printing was now the uppermost

in my thoughts, and hackney authors began to ply me with *specimens* as earnestly and with as much passion and concern as the watermen do passengers with *Oars* and *Scullers*. I had some acquaintance with this generation in my apprenticeship, and had never any warm affection for them, in regard I always thought their great concern lay more in *how much a sheet*, than in any generous respect they bore to the *Commonwealth of Learning*; and indeed the learning itself of these gentlemen lies very often in as little room as their honesty, though they will pretend to have studied for six or seven years in the Bodleian Library, to have turned over the Fathers, and to have read and digested the whole compass both of human and ecclesiastic history, when, alas! they have never been able to understand a single page of St. Cyprian, and cannot tell you whether the Fathers lived before or after Christ."

Yet of one of this hateful tribe Dunton is able to speak well. He declares Mr. Bradshaw to have been the best accomplished hackney author he ever met with. He pronounces his style incomparably fine. He had quarrelled with him, but none the less he writes: " If Mr. Bradshaw is yet alive, I here declare to the world and to him that I freely forgive him what he owes, both in money and books, if he will only be so kind as to make me a visit. But I am afraid the worthy gentleman is dead, for he was wretchedly overrun with melancholy, and the very blackness of it reigned in his countenance. He had certainly performed wonders with his pen, had not his poverty pursued him and almost laid the necessity upon him to be unjust."

All hackney authors were not poor. Some of the compilers and abridgers made what even now would be considered by popular novelists large sums. Scotsmen were very good at it. Gordon and Campbell became wealthy men. If authors had a turn for politics, Sir Robert Walpole was an excellent paymaster. Arnall, who was bred an attorney, is stated to have been paid £11,000 in four years by the Government for his pamphlets.

> " Come, then, I'll comply,
> Spirit of Arnall, aid me while I lie!"

It cannot have been pleasant to read this, but then Pope belonged to the opposition, and was a friend of Lord Bolingbroke, and would consequently say anything.

There is not a more interesting and artless autobiography to be read than William Hutton's, the famous bookseller and historian of Birmingham. Hutton has been somewhat absurdly called the English Franklin. He is not in the least like Franklin. He has none of Franklin's supreme literary skill, and he was a loving, generous, and tender-hearted man, which Franklin certainly was not. Hutton's first visit to London was paid in 1749. He walked up from Nottingham, spent three days in London, and then walked back to Nottingham. The jaunt, if such an expression is applicable, cost him eleven shillings less fourpence. Yet he paid his way. The only money he spent to gain admission to public places was a penny to see Bedlam.

Interesting, however, as is Hutton's book, it tells us next to nothing about book-selling, except that in his hands it was a prosperous undertaking.

EDWARD VERRALL LUCAS

(1868–1938)

E. V. Lucas spent his early life as a journalist and reporter. His talent, however, developed in the direction of the light essay, and in 1902 he joined the staff of *Punch*. He also wrote a few novels and some verse, but it was as an essayist that he gained a place in the world of literature. His work has probably more in common with that of Lamb than the work of any other modern essayist.

HER ROYAL 'TUMNAL TINTINESS

She is absurdly small — a homœopathic dose of a dog. Nothing but the folly of Western fashions prevents her from being carried in the sleeve, as Nature and Art intended her to be. But she is small only in figure; in all else she is as large as a Newfoundland — in fidelity and courage and spirit and protectiveness and appetite (proportionately), and love of ease — while in brain power she is larger. Although not six months old, she has the gravity of age, she suggests complete mental maturity. If she were ten she could not open an eye upon a superfluous caress with more languor or disdain. Her regality is such that one resorts to all kinds of expedients to win her favour. She has the more radiant merits of the cat — she eats like a cat, with all its meticulous cleanliness and precision, she plays with a cotton-reel like a cat, she has a cat's flexibility in her toilet. On your knee she sinks into complacency like a cat.

None the less she is a true dog too, with nearly all the stigmata of her kind — the black muzzle, the deep stop, the flat forehead, the plumed tail carried high, the bowed legs, the minuteness, the nervous fluid. Her hue is that of a beech leaf in autumn.

When she runs from room to room she beats the floor with her forepaws with a gallant little rocking-horse action. When she runs over grass she makes a russet streak like a hare, with the undulating ripple of a sea-serpent, and her soft pads reverberate like muffled hoofs. When she is not running she is asleep. When she sleeps the most comfortable place in the room is hopelessly engaged until she wakes. However fast she may be sleeping, she wakes directly her particular friend leaves the room, her religion being sociability. Left alone she screams. Put out of the house alone, she circumnavigates it with the speed of thought, seeking an open door or window. The sunlight through her tongue is more than rubies.

One difficulty that seems to confront many owners of Pekingese spaniels is the finding of a suitable name; for it should of course be Chinese and also easily pronounceable. But to those who have the honour to possess Professor Giles's " Chinese Biographical Dictionary " the situation is without such complications. Turning over its pages I quickly alighted upon a choice of engaging females whose names might fitly be conferred upon Her Autumn Leafiness. To mention a few, there is A-chiao, who, when a child, was shown to the Emperor Wu Ti, also a child, and he was asked what he thought of her as a possible wife. " Oh," said the boy, " if I could get A-chiao I would have a golden house to keep her in." There is Chao Fie-yen, who was so graceful and light that she was called " Flying Swallow ". There is Chao Yün, who died with these words from the " Diamond Lutra " on her lips: " Like a dream, like a vision, like a bubble, like a shadow, like dew, like lightning." There is Ch'i Nu, who had two lovers, one of which lived on the right of the house and the other on the left. Her father bade her tuck up the sleeve which corresponded to the man whom she preferred, and she tucked up both, saying that she would like to live with the handsome one and eat with the rich. (This dog is very like that.) There is Féng Hou, one of the favourites of the Emperor Yüan Ti, who, when a bear escaped, did not flee with all the other ladies, but remained to face the bear, saying: " I was afraid lest some harm should come to Your Majesty's person." There is Hsi Chih, who was never so lovely as when she knitted her brows; and P'an Fei, the favourite of Hsiao Pao-chüan, who said of her, " Every step makes a lily grow!" and Pei Ch'i Kung Chu, who awakened in the breast of her lover such a flame that it set fire to a temple; and Tao Yün, who when her brother likened a snow-storm to salt sprinkled in the air, corrected the feebleness of his simile by comparing it to willow-catkins whirled by the wind; and Ts'ai Luan, who compiled a rhyming dictionary and ascended to heaven with her husband, each on a white tiger. Here, you observe, is a considerable range — although by no means all — for the selecting mind to consider.

The choice fell upon Féng Hou. That is the name to which, since it is hers and she is all caprice and individuality, she refuses to answer.

> The dog will come when he is called,
> The cat will turn away.

— so wrote an old observer. It is true of dogs and cats, but it is hopelessly amiss of Pekingese. I would amend it thus:

> The dog will come when he is called,
>   The cat will turn away;
> The Pekingese will please itself,
>   Whatever you may say.

For, to adapt an old proverb, where there's a Pekingese there's a will.

I do not think that she is ever likely to be a wonder from the point of view of the bench. At least one of the dreaded penalizations is hers already, and she may acquire others; nothing can make her fit to sit beside her illustrious grandfather, Ch. Chu'erh of Alderbourne, that Napoleon of Pekingese, that Meredith, that Brummell, all combined; nor has she the ingratiating pictorial charm of Ch. Broadoak Beetle; but no one knows what her own children may be like, and meanwhile she is enough for her owner. She has brought into a house hitherto unconscious of it the delectable piquancy of Peking.

Having done all that was possible to make Féng Hou our own, no one in the house having any independent will left, and butcher's bills rising like Grahame White: having done all this, it was something more than a shock to be favoured with a translation of the rhapsodical pearls of wisdom dropped from the lips of her Imperial Majesty Tzŭ Hsi, the late Dowager Empress of Western China, for the guidance of the master of her kennel. One saw at once how much was still to do if Féng Hou was to be worthy of her race. I quote this most delightful document, the very flower of Chinese solicitude and fancy.

PEARLS DROPPED FROM THE LIPS OF
HER IMPERIAL MAJESTY, TZŬ HSI,
DOWAGER EMPRESS OF THE FLOWERY LAND

Let the Lion Dog be small: let it wear the swelling cape of dignity around its neck: let it display the billowing standard of pomp above its back.

Let its face be black: let its fore-legs be shaggy: let its forehead be straight and low, like unto the brow of an Imperial righteous harmony boxer.

Let its eyes be large and luminous: let its ears be set like the sails of a war-junk: let its nose be like that of the monkey god of the Hindus.

Let its fore-legs be bent, so that it shall not desire to wander far, or leave the Imperial precincts.

Let its body be shaped like that of a hunting lion spying for its prey.

Let its feet be tufted with plentiful hair that its footfall may be soundless: and for its standard of pomp let it rival the whisk of the Tibetan's yak, which is flourished to protect the Imperial litter from the attacks of flying insects.

Let it be lively that it may afford entertainment by its gambols; let it be timid that it may not involve itself in danger; let it be domestic in its habits that it may live in amity with the other beasts, fishes, or birds that find protection in the Imperial Palace. And for its colour, let it be that of the lion — a golden sable, to be carried in the sleeve of a yellow robe, or the colour of a red bear, or a black or a white bear, or striped like a dragon, so that there may be dogs appropriate to every costume in the Imperial wardrobe.

Let it venerate its ancestors and deposit offerings in the canine cemetery of the Forbidden City on each new moon.

Let it comport itself with dignity; let it learn to bite the foreign devils instantly.

Let it be dainty in its food that it shall be known for an Imperial dog by its fastidiousness.

Sharks' fins and curlews' livers and the breasts of quails, on these it may be fed; and for drink give it the tea that is brewed from the spring buds of the shrub that groweth in the province of the Hankow, or the milk of the antelopes that pasture in the Imperial parks. Thus shall it preserve its integrity and self-respect; and for the day of sickness let it be anointed with the clarified fat of the leg of a sacred leopard, and give it to drink a throstle's egg-shell full of the juice of the custard-apple in which have been dissolved three pinches of shredded rhinoceros horn, and apply to it piebald leeches.

So shall it remain; but if it die, remember thou, too, art mortal.

That is a very charming poem, is it not? Queen Victoria drew up no such rules for Dandie Dinmonts, nor did Charles I, so far as I know, thus establish the standard of the little creatures with whose ears he played instead of studying the signs of the times. But it must necessarily strike some apprehension into the breast of the owner of a Pekingese. Is one doing rightly by the dog? is a question that it forces upon one. In the matter of diet alone I find that we have been all to seek. No house could have been so free from sharks' fins and curlews' livers as this, and if a quail's breast has chanced to enter, it was certainly not Féng Hou who ate it. As for drink — but I wonder if anyone can recommend me a good, trustworthy antelope milker: one who would not object to help in the garden when it is not milking-time? Things would be simple then — until Féng Hou was ill. But that does not bear thinking about.

Apropos of medicine, however, an odd thing happened. Féng Hou at first was not always good; indeed she was sometimes extremely naughty; and a little castigating seemed needful. A letter therefore was dispatched to London, to a provider of quaint necessaries, asking that some attractive little switch, worthy of such a creature, might be supplied. It came at once — the most delicate and radiant of rods, with a note saying that it was something of a curiosity, being pure rhinoceros horn. So we have one of the ingredients of one of the prescriptions after all! Physic indeed.

JOSEPH HILAIRE PIERRE BELLOC

(born 1870)

Hilaire Belloc was born in France, went to school in England, performed military service with the French army, and then went to Balliol College. He became a British subject in 1902. He has been journalist, essayist, poet, and novelist; and he also gained fame as a military critic during the Great War. A man of distinguished style and very wide interests, he has written upon almost every conceivable subject.

ON CHEESES

If antiquity be the test of nobility, as many affirm and none deny (saving, indeed, that family which takes for its motto " Sola Virtus Nobilitas ", which may mean that virtue is the only nobility, but which may also mean, mark you, that nobility is the only virtue — and anyhow denies that nobility is tested by the lapse of time), *if,* I say, antiquity be the only test of nobility, then cheese is a very noble thing.

But wait a moment: there was a digression in that first paragraph which to the purist might seem of a complicated kind.

Were I writing algebra (I wish I were) I could have analysed my thoughts by the use of square brackets, round brackets, twiddly brackets, and the rest, all properly set out in order so that a Common Fool could follow them.

But no such luck! I may not write of algebra here;

for there is a rule current in all newspapers that no man may write upon any matter save upon those in which he is more learned than all his human fellows that drag themselves so slowly daily forward to the grave.

So I had to put the thing in the very common form of a digression, and very nearly forgot that great subject of cheese which I had put at the very head and title of this.

Which reminds me; had I followed the rule set down by a London journalist the other day (and of the proprietor of his paper I will say nothing — though I might have put down the remark to his proprietor) I would have hesitated to write that first paragraph. I would have hesitated, did I say? Griffins' tails! Nay — Hippogriffs and other things of the night! I would not have dared to write it at all. For this journalist made a law and promulgated it, and the law was this: that no man should write that English which could not be understood if all the punctuation were left out. Punctuation, I take it, includes brackets, which the Lord of Printers knows are a very modern part of punctuation indeed.

Now let the horripilised reader look up again at the first paragraph (it will do him no harm), and think how it would look all written out in fair uncials like the beautiful Gospels of St. Chad, which anyone may see for nothing in the cathedral of Lichfield, an English town famous for eight or nine different things: as Garrick, Doctor Johnson, and its two opposite inns. Come, read that first paragraph over now and see what you could make of it if it were written out in uncials — that is, not only without punctuation, but without any division between the words. Wow! As the philosopher said when he was asked to give a plain answer " Yes " or " No ".

And now to cheese. I have had quite enough of digressions and of follies. They are the happy youth of an article. They are the springtime of it. They are its riot. I am approaching the middle age of this article. Let us be solid upon the matter of cheese.

I have premised its antiquity, which is of two sorts, as is that of a nobleman. First, the antiquity of its lineage; secondly, the antiquity of its self. For we all know that when we meet a nobleman we revere his nobility very much if he be himself old, and that this quality of age in him seems to marry itself in some mysterious way with the antiquity of his line.

The lineage of cheese is demonstrably beyond all record. What did the faun in the beginning of time when a god surprised him or a mortal had the misfortune to come across him in the woods? It is well known that the faun offered either of them cheese. So he knew how to make it.

There are certain bestial men, hangers-on of the Germans, who would contend that this would prove cheese to be acquired by the Aryan race (or what not) from the Dolichocephalics (or what not), and there are certain horrors who descend to imitate these barbarians — though themselves born in these glorious islands, which are so steep upon their western side. But I will not detain you upon these lest I should fall head foremost into another digression and forget that my article, already in its middle age, is now approaching grey hairs.

At any rate, cheese is very old. It is beyond written language. Whether it is older than butter has been exhaustively discussed by several learned men, to whom I do not send you because the road towards them leads elsewhere. It is the universal opinion of all most accus-

tomed to weigh evidence (and in these I very properly
include not only such political hacks as are already
upon the bench but sweepingly every single lawyer in
Parliament, since any of them may to-morrow be a
judge) that milk is older than cheese, and that man had
the use of milk before he cunningly devised the trick of
squeezing it in a press and by sacrificing something of
its sweetness endowed it with a sort of immortality.

The story of all this has perished. Do not believe any
man who professes to give it you. If he tells you some
legend of a god who taught the Wheat-eating race, the
Ploughers, and the Lords to make cheese, tell him such
tales are true symbols, but symbols only. If he tells you
that cheese was an evolution and a development, oh!
then! — bring up your guns! Open on the fellow and
sweep his intolerable lack of intelligence from the earth.
Ask him if he discovers reality to be a function of time,
and Being to hide in clockwork. Keep him on the hop
with ironical comments upon how it may be that environment can act upon Will, while Will can do nothing
with environment — whose proper name is mud. Pester
the provincial. Run him off the field.

But about cheese. Its noble antiquity breeds in it a
noble diffusion.

This happy Christendom of ours (which is just now
suffering from an indigestion and needs a doctor — but
having also a complication of insomnia cannot recollect
his name) has been multifarious incredibly — but in
nothing more than in cheese!

One cheese differs from another, and the difference
is in sweeps, and in landscapes, and in provinces, and in
countrysides, and in climates, and in principalities, and
in realms, and in the nature of things. Cheese does most

gloriously reflect the multitudinous effect of earthly things, which could not be multitudinous did they not proceed from one mind.

Consider the cheese of Rocquefort: how hard it is in its little box. Consider the cheese of Camembert, which is hard also, and also lives in a little box, but must not be eaten until it is soft and yellow. Consider the cheese of Stilton, which is not made there, and of Cheddar, which is. Then there is your Parmesan, which idiots buy rancid in bottles, but which the wise grate daily for their use: you think it is hard from its birth? You are mistaken. It is the world that hardens the Parmesan. In its youth the Parmesan is very soft and easy, and is voraciously devoured.

Then there is your cheese of Wensleydale, which is made in Wensleydale, and your little Swiss cheese, which is soft and creamy and eaten with sugar, and there is your Cheshire cheese and your little Cornish cheese, whose name escapes me, and your huge round cheese out of the Midlands, as big as a fort whose name I never heard. There is your toasted or Welsh cheese, and your cheese of Pont-l'évèque, and your white cheese of Brie, which is a chalky sort of cheese. And there is your cheese of Neufchâtel, and there is your Gorgonzola cheese, which is mottled all over like some marbles, or like that Mediterranean soap which is made of wood-ash and of olive oil. There is your Gloucester cheese called the Double Gloucester, and I have read in a book of Dunlop Cheese, which is made in Ayrshire: they could tell you more about it in Kilmarnock. Then Suffolk makes a cheese, but does not give it any name; and talking of that reminds me how going to Le Quesnoy to pass the people there the time of day, and to see what

was left of that famous but forgotten fortress, a young
man there showed me a cheese, which he told me also
had no name, but which was native to the town, and in
the valley of Ste. Engrace, where is that great wood
which shuts off all the world, they make their cheese of
ewe's milk and sell it in Tardets, which is their only
livelihood. They make a cheese in Port Salut which is
a very subtle cheese, and there is a cheese of Limburg,
and I know not how many others, or rather I know them,
but you have had enough: for a little cheese goes a long
way. No man is a glutton on cheese.

What other cheese has great holes in it like Gruyere,
or what other is as round as a cannon-ball like that
cheese called Dutch? which reminds me: —

Talking of Dutch cheese. Do you not notice how the
intimate mind of Europe is reflected in cheese? For in
the centre of Europe, and where Europe is most active,
I mean in Britain and in Gaul and in Northern Italy,
and in the valley of the Rhine — nay, to some extent
in Spain (in her Pyrenean valleys at least) — there
flourishes a vast burgeoning of cheese, infinite in variety,
one in goodness. But as Europe fades away under the
African wound which Spain suffered or the Eastern
barbarism of the Elbe, what happens to cheese? It
becomes very flat and similar. You can quote six cheeses
perhaps which the public power of Christendom has
founded outside the limits of its ancient Empire — but
not more than six. I will quote you 253 between the
Ebro and the Grampians, between Brindisi and the
Irish Channel.

I do not write vainly. It is a profound thing.

GILBERT KEITH CHESTERTON

(1874–1936)

Essayist, novelist, humorist, poet, and artist, Chesterton had a keen sense of humour and the ridiculous and a great love of paradox; the latter appears particularly in his detective stories. Like his friend Hilaire Belloc, he wrote on almost every possible subject, always with striking originality.

ON RUNNING AFTER ONE'S HAT

I feel an almost savage envy on hearing that London has been flooded in my absence, while I am in the mere country. My own Battersea has been, I understand, particularly favoured as a meeting of the waters. Battersea was already, as I need hardly say, the most beautiful of human localities. Now that it has the additional splendour of great sheets of water, there must be something quite incomparable in the landscape (or waterscape) of my own romantic town. Battersea must be a vision of Venice. The boat that brought the meat from the butcher's must have shot along those lanes of rippling silver with the strange smoothness of the gondola. The greengrocer who brought cabbages to the corner of the Latchmere Road must have leant upon the oar with the unearthly grace of the gondolier. There is nothing so perfectly poetical as an island; and when a district is flooded it becomes an archipelago.

Some consider such romantic views of flood or fire

slightly lacking in reality. But really this romantic view of such inconveniences is quite as practical as the other. The true optimist who sees in such things an opportunity for enjoyment is quite as logical and much more sensible than the ordinary " Indignant Ratepayer " who sees in them an opportunity for grumbling. Real pain, as in the case of being burnt at Smithfield or having a toothache, is a positive thing; it can be supported, but scarcely enjoyed. But, after all, our toothaches are the exception, and as for being burnt at Smithfield, it only happens to us at the very longest intervals. And most of the inconveniences that make men swear or women cry are really sentimental or imaginative inconveniences — things altogether of the mind. For instance, we often hear grown-up people complaining of having to hang about a railway station and wait for a train. Did you ever hear a small boy complain of having to hang about a railway station and wait for a train? No; for to him to be inside a railway station is to be inside a cavern of wonder and a palace of poetical pleasures. Because to him the red light and the green light on the signal are like a new sun and a new moon. Because to him when the wooden arm of the signal falls down suddenly, it is as if a great king had thrown down his staff as a signal and started a shrieking tournament of trains. I myself am of little boys' habit in this matter. They also serve who only stand and wait for the two fifteen. Their meditations may be full of rich and fruitful things. Many of the most purple hours of my life have been passed at Clapham Junction, which is now, I suppose, under water. I have been there in many moods so fixed and mystical that the water might well have come up to my waist before I noticed it particularly. But in the case of all such annoyances, as I have said, everything depends upon the emotional point of view. You can safely apply the test to almost every one of the things that are currently talked of as the typical nuisance of daily life.

For instance, there is a current impression that it is unpleasant to have to run after one's hat. Why should it be unpleasant to the well-ordered and pious mind? Not merely because it is running, and running exhausts one. The same people run much faster in games and sports. The same people run much more eagerly after an uninteresting little leather ball than they will after a nice silk hat. There is an idea that it is humiliating to run after one's hat; and when people say it is humiliating they mean that it is comic. It certainly is comic; but man is a very comic creature, and most of the things he does are comic — eating, for instance. And the most comic things of all are exactly the things that are most worth doing — such as making love. A man running after a hat is not half so ridiculous as a man running after a wife.

Now a man could, if he felt rightly in the matter, run after his hat with the manliest ardour and the most sacred joy. He might regard himself as a jolly huntsman pursuing a wild animal, for certainly no animal could be wilder. In fact, I am inclined to believe that hat-hunting on windy days will be the sport of the upper classes in the future. There will be a meet of ladies and gentlemen on some high ground on a gusty morning. They will be told that the professional attendants have started a hat in such-and-such a thicket, or whatever be the technical term. Notice that this employment will in the fullest degree combine sport with humanitarianism. The

hunters would feel that they were not inflicting pain.
Nay, they would feel that they were inflicting pleasure,
rich, almost riotous pleasure, upon the people who were
looking on. When last I saw an old gentleman running
after his hat in Hyde Park, I told him that a heart so
benevolent as his ought to be filled with peace and thanks
at the thought of how much unaffected pleasure his
every gesture and bodily attitude were at that moment
giving to the crowd.

The same principle can be applied to every other
typical domestic worry. A gentleman trying to get a fly
out of the milk or a piece of cork out of his glass of wine
often imagines himself to be irritated. Let him think
for a moment of the patience of anglers sitting by dark
pools, and let his soul be immediately irradiated with
gratification and repose. Again, I have known some
people of very modern views driven by their distress
to the use of theological terms to which they attached
no doctrinal significance, merely because a drawer was
jammed tight and they could not pull it out. A friend
of mine was particularly afflicted in this way. Every day
his drawer was jammed, and every day in consequence
it was something else that rhymes to it. But I pointed
out to him that this sense of wrong was really subjective
and relative; it rested entirely upon the assumption
that the drawer could, should, and would come out
easily. " But if," I said, " you picture to yourself that
you are pulling against some powerful and oppressive
enemy, the struggle will become merely exciting and
not exasperating. Imagine that you are tugging up a
lifeboat out of the sea. Imagine that you are roping up
a fellow-creature out of an Alpine crevasse. Imagine
even that you are a boy again and engaged in a tug-of-

war between French and English." Shortly after saying this I left him; but I have no doubt at all that my words bore the best possible fruit. I have no doubt that every day of his life he hangs on to the handle of that drawer with a flushed face and eyes bright with battle, uttering encouraging shouts to himself, and seeming to hear all round him the roar of an applauding ring.

So I do not think that it is altogether fanciful or incredible to suppose that even the floods in London may be accepted and enjoyed poetically. Nothing beyond inconvenience seems really to have been caused by them; and inconvenience, as I have said, is only one aspect, and that the most unimaginative and accidental aspect of a really romantic situation. An adventure is only an inconvenience rightly considered. An inconvenience is only an adventure wrongly considered. The water that girdled the houses and shops of London must, if anything, have only increased their previous witchery and wonder. For as the Roman Catholic priest in the story said: " Wine is good with everything except water," and on a similar principle, water is good with everything except wine.

ROBERT LYND

(born 1879)

Like some of the other writers in this book, Lynd was born in Ireland, and much of what he has written deals with Ireland. He was for many years the literary editor of the *News Chronicle*, and has published several books of essays, many of them light, others critical. As this essay shows, he is a keen student of Nature. His wife, Sylvia Lynd, is also a writer.

THE UNEXPECTED

There usually comes a Saturday in May when I feel an intense longing to hear a nightingale. It is not that the nightingale brings back old associations or conjures back the vision of a happy childhood, for I was born in a country in which no nightingale ever sings and in which the nightingale is as much a bird of the imagination as the phœnix. Still, if you had been reading about the phœnix all your life, and if at last after many years you saw a real phœnix, would you not be more excited than if you had been surrounded by phœnixes since your infancy? It is not easy to say whether the fascination of the creatures we have always known or the creatures we have only heard about and wondered about is the greater. The one in the end, perhaps, becomes over-familiar while the other remains as unfamiliar as a legend. I find that, as I grow older, familiar creatures such as hens and pigs do not seem as wonderful as they used to seem. As a child, I was not content till I not only knew the family name of each hen on the farm that was my second home — Dorking or Leghorn or Cochin China — but had given all the most interesting of the birds Christian names or nicknames. To-day, I find hens rather depressing company, slaves content with their slavery, incapable of oddity (as a duck is capable of it), birds that have all but lost the power of flight, and interesting only in the flurried defence of their young. Yet once I would rather have visited a henhouse than have gone to the circus. The scent of a room in which hens had awakened from their sleep, which I now find odious, was to me better than the smell of honey-suckle. To a town child, indeed, the farm in those days was a legend — every horse as marvellous as a unicorn, the cows as astonishing as dragons, and the bull mag-nificent in his strength as Behemoth. But all that has faded. The animals on the farm are no longer legends, but captives, doing, like oneself, more or less useful work.

On the other hand, if I had never seen a hen till I was middle-aged, I am sure I should still be able to regard it through the eyes of wonder. If it were a bird known only in some old myth of Greece or Rome — a queen metamorphosed or the attendant bird of a goddess — how mysteriously beautiful it would seem! There would be myths of the heroism of hens, of their cruel beaks, and of the various and lovely pattern of their feathers. The hen would appear in crests as often as the pelican — an image of piety and self-sacrifice. Even the goose has retained some of its ancient dignity because it figures in a Roman legend. It is a bird that has played a part in great affairs, and still seems unresigned to its fate as a drudge on a farm. Perhaps the fact that in childhood we are a little afraid of it helps to preserve our respect for it through life. It is impossible to treat a gander or, indeed, a turkey-cock as though it did not exist. They are never entirely domesticated and tamed to the dull services of the table. The hen, however, has lost the last traces of rebelliousness, and toils for us sulkily without spirit and without protest. If she purred like a cat, or wagged her tail like a dog, we could still take some interest in her, but her behaviour forces us to the fancy, — a ridiculous fancy, probably — that hens have no souls.

None of the wild birds disappoints us in this fashion in later life. They are free, or at least they seem to be free. Even the city sparrow does not work for a master; it may be a parasite, but it is not a drudge. To the townsman, indeed, most of the birds remain half-legendary to the end. He has no command over their comings or their goings. If they wish to go to Africa, they go to Africa. If they wish to be silent, they cease singing. He may put up nesting-boxes for them in his garden, but he cannot compel them to lay their eggs in them. If there is any relationship of slavery between man and the wild bird, it is the bird-lover that is the slave of the bird, not the bird that is the slave of the bird-lover. He is interested in it; it has no interest in him except to avoid him. He may search for it for years, but it will never search for him. It may make use of his garden, eat his young peas, and devour his raspberries, but it feels no more indebted to him than a Highland chieftain felt to the Lowlander whose cattle he raided. It is true that birds are occasionally put into cages, and that goldfinches have even been known to show affection for those who have imprisoned them; but the wild bird in its natural state scarcely recognizes the existence of the human race. The robin may perch on the gardener's spade, but it is for its own purposes. It looks on the gardener as its own private gardener who turns up the earth for it — a slave under its eye cultivating its worm-farm without fee or reward.

Hence we never lose our respect for wild birds. Their attitude to us is aristocratic, and, even if we regard them as enemies, we do not despise them. Many a man with an orchard has murdered a bullfinch, but no one has ever thought meanly of a bullfinch. You may swear at the hawfinch that empties the pods of your peas, but you are not indifferent to him. You may resent the blackbird's raids on your raspberries, and may even spread nets against him, but you would no more think of looking down on a blackbird than of looking down on Dick Turpin. And, of all the birds that compel respect and interest the imagination, the most compulsive and interesting are those who come when they will and go when they will — who may endure us through the pleasures of summer but resolutely refuse to share with us the rudeness of winter. Owing to this, they preserve the perpetual charm of strangers. Every year the return of the unfamiliar swallow fills us with delight like the coming of a visitor from Paradise. Even the monotonous repetitions of the chiffchaff bring Africa and all its pro-digies into the apple-tree in the garden. There may be songs as sweet sung by the birds that stay at home, but no other song seems as sweet to us as the songs of these returned prodigals. If the whitethroat were an island bird that began to sing in February, we should not so enjoy its dangle of wings in the air and the harsh, disapproving notes of its song. But any bird that brings back the summer is a noble bird, and transforms the earth from a dull plain into a polling star. The fact that more poets have addressed their verses to the wren, the thrush, and the blackbird may seem to disprove this; but I fancy that many of the poets, knowing very little about ornithology, have given the birds names at random, and have often addressed to the linnet lines that, if they had known better, would have been addressed to the willow-wren. I have but a small gift of prophecy, but I venture to prophesy that, if ever another Shakespeare appears in England, there will be a song to the willow-wren among his lyrics.

If the nightingale is supreme among the birds of all kinds, it is because not only is it a wild bird like the chaffinch and a bird that comes and goes as it pleases like the willow-wren, but it remains for most people a legend — remote and mysterious as the Holy Grail. It is probable that three-quarters of the inhabitants of these islands have never heard a nightingale except over the wireless. For them it may have a miraculous beauty that was never yet achieved in song, and if, hearing it over the wireless, they are a little disappointed, they put the blame not on the bird but on the wireless. They know that the beauty of a bird consists not only on its song but in its surroundings. They feel that notes precipitated from a loud speaker cannot be quite the same thing as a song issuing from a white throat on which the moonlight falls through the leaves. It is, I admit, possible that some people are disappointed on hearing for the first time a nightingale singing under a May moon. There are people who are capable of being disappointed in anything, as Wilde was disappointed in the

Atlantic Ocean. There was an American poet who came to England some years ago and who, having read and loved Shelley's " Skylark ", longed above all things to hear a skylark singing. She got her wish, and she wished that she had not. In bitter disappointment she went back to America and wrote a poem to the skylark in which she addressed it reproachfully:

> Thou didst not sing to Shelley half so sweet
> A song as Shelley sang to thee.

That, I think, was the result of expecting a bird to perform like an operatic tenor — to produce music that would delight the ear with its brilliance apart from any riches of association. Birds' songs are certainly not to be enjoyed in this fashion. The bird's song is not only music, but the voice of the air, the tree or the countryside. You cannot expect to enjoy a bird's song if you go out to hear it in the same spirit in which you go out to see the face in the rocks at Land's End. If you do, the prose of the guide-book will enter into your soul. I am sure that the greatest pleasure to be got from the song of birds is pleasure that is not sought out but comes unexpectedly and unasked for. Half the pleasures of the woods and fields are for those who take things as they come — who know that legends are hidden among the leaves and for whom, if a nightingale does happen to sing, it is as if a legend had in an incredible fashion come true.

Though I know this, I confess I went into the country the other day deliberately in order to hear the nightingale. I went to a valley where I have never failed to hear the nightingale in May for several years past, even when sleet was falling, and where I have taken other men to one particular copse to hear the nightingale as confidently as you would take a man to see the Poets' Corner in Westminster Abbey. Yet, whether the drought was unpropitious to song, or whether the robbers of nests have diminished the population of the nightingales, no bush became on fire with the accustomed voice. The wood-wren and the willow-wren, the tree-creeper and the long-tailed tit, the jay and the great spotted woodpecker, the nuthatch and the garden-warbler — half the family of the birds were there living their lives in the old fashion, but the nightingale was only the memory of a legend.

On the whole, however, I do not complain. Nature would not be so charming if she had not such a gift for the unexpected. And if at times she disappoints our expectations, she is just as likely to delight us with unexpected novelties. On this day, I confess, I was delighted when, as I lay under a hedge expecting nothing, a lapwing came into the field, crest nobly erect, followed by her — or his — two little chickens that ran about the grass feeding at a greater and greater distance from their apprehensive parent. I had never seen the chickens of a lapwing before, and, as they ran about with the little white patches on the back of their necks, the whole world was transformed into a nursery, and I would not have missed the spectacle for a hundred nightingales. When at length I rose and crossed the stile out of the field, the lapwing flew after me, screaming above the hedge, and returning again and again to make sure that I had gone. Her fears and her chickens filled me with sentimental thoughts with which I will not trouble you. You have all had them when looking at ducklings or calves or foals, or at the human young when learning to walk.

EDMUND GEORGE VALPY KNOX

(born 1881)

Journalist, essayist, and humorist, E. V. Knox joined the staff of *Punch* in 1921, and succeeded Sir Owen Seaman as the editor of that periodical in 1932. He is a writer with a gentle but incisive humour and a very clear, simple style. He has written novels as well as essays, and also some verse.

WITCHES AND WHATNOT

There is a recent tendency in English literature which I find a little peculiar. It is not so much a frank, open-minded tolerance of witchcraft, voodooism, magical rites, incantations, and heathen sacrifice such as might be expected from persons of intellect and culture. It is more than that. It is a desire to plunge into these things and wallow in their midst; to take part in the rites of oboi and gaga, to collect herbs under the moonlight and make soup with them, to practise in very truth the mysteries of the old Incas of Peru and the old Iguanas of Honduras; to make one's way into the most difficult jungles of Central Africa or Central America, tattoo oneself all over, put a ring through one's nose, and, if possible, to lap blood.

There is a distinct change here between our present attitude and that of Victorian literature. Victorian literature, on the whole, was inclined to censure the heathen in his blindness for bowing down to wood and stone. Or, if not, it took the even colder attitude of censuring people for bowing down to any kind of deity whatever. An earnest advocacy of demoniac dances, a bigoted belief in witch-doctors breathes through the pages of none of the great poets or novelists of those bygone days. But now it is quite otherwise.

At any moment, I gather, a young girl may start up and say to her mother, " I am tired of this feverish and outworn civilization. I am going out and away to the far places of Mexico to find a strong, vivid, brown-limbed people who practise the old faith of the Mayas. I mean to wander amongst them until they take me away into the mountain fastnesses and drug me with strange herbs, and then at last lead me to the sacrificial chamber. And there, at the moment when the shaft of the sun strikes the altar, they will lay me on the cold stone and sacrifice me, and I shall know a completeness and a contentedness beyond imagination, and beyond dream."

" Yes, dear," says her mother; " when do you want to start?"

" This very afternoon."

" I wish you could put it off till to-morrow, dear, because the Smiths are coming to-night, and I hoped you would arrange the flowers for dinner."

But the young girl is obdurate, and goes to look up the rail and steamer services to Popocatepetl at once.

Just as she starts, her mother, moist-eyed, presses into her hands a hot-water bottle with a knitted cover, for she cannot help feeling how cold it will be out there on the sacrificial stone amongst the Maya priests and priestesses.

" Of course I know the child must arrange her own life," she murmurs to herself as the taxicab departs for Waterloo.

Or another young girl will say quite suddenly at breakfast:

" By the way, Dad, I have decided to become a witch."

" Oh, yes," says her father, frowning a little over the top of *The Times*. " When do you want to begin?"

" Almost at once. I thought of getting a few toads together to-day and buying some simples and a one-eyed cat. I've seen a heavenly little cottage down in Hertfordshire that would be just the thing, and I want you to buy it for me, please."

" You won't make much of a living out of it, will you?" he grumbles, as he adjusts his spectacles and writes out the cheque.

" Oh, but of course I shall, Dad. I shall make little wax images to stick through with pins for people who want to put evil spells on their neighbours, and I shall brew hell-broths and love-philtres, and cure people's rheumatism by making ointment from mouse-fat for them. I can have no end of a good time."

" Very well, then," he growls. " Wilkins will take you down in the Daimler."

And off she goes too.

And now, last of all, I find the book of a man who has penetrated to the very centre of Haiti, and shared with really simple faith and enthusiasm in the fine old secret orgies of Voodoo, which those of our ancestors who knew anything about them always thought were things to be discouraged as compared with muscular Christianity and cold morning baths.

The author is a Mr. W. B. Seabrook, who, it appears, has done very good work previously in Arabia amongst the Bedouins and Druses, and whirling dervishes and

devil-worshippers. But he has done better, I should
say, in Haiti. He saw some really jolly religious cere-
monies out there.

" In the actual slaying of the sacrificial beasts which
now began, accompanied by deep chanting, there was
no savagery, no needless cruelty, no lust of killing. It
was a solemn ritual business, though, when once it
began, it moved swiftly. A goat was held by the horns,
the sharp-edged *machete* drawn across the throat by a
papeloi, and the blood gushed into a wooden bowl. . . .
And the bull, before whom, deified, the blood of these
other beasts had been poured out as an offering, must
also die. . . . The blood did not gush fountain-like, as
it had from the cut throats of the goats; it spurted in
a hard, small stream from the bull's pierced side. . . .
The *papeloi* and *mameloi* now both drank ceremonially
of the holy blood, and then, amid the crescendo excitement and surging forward of the worshippers, the twenty
women robed in white danced in a group, leaping and
whirling like frenzied maenads. . . . It was savage and
abandoned, but it seemed to me magnificent and not
devoid of a certain beauty. Something inside myself
awoke and responded to it."

It would. That is always the way it happens in these
modern books. Something very deep and innate, and
primitive and holy stirs in the heart of the watcher as
soon as the knife-slashing and yelling and eyeball rolling begin, and they feel that all is right in the best of
possible worlds.

After that Mr. Seabrook saw another ceremony, where
the spirit of a girl passed magically into " a sturdy brown
young goat with big blue, terrified, almost human eyes ",
and then the goat was killed and its blood passed round.

" So the bowl itself was held to my lips, and three times I drank. The blood had a clean, warm, salty taste."

That causes me no particular surprise. Any one who has had a tooth knocked out will have discovered this without having gone to Haiti. But the point is that Mr. Seabrook liked it. He says so.

He does more. He writes in another place: " That human sacrifice occurs in Voodoo to-day may seem strange and, to many persons, horrible. But only, I think, because they consider it in terms of ' time '. With the time-element removed, and considered in terms of space, religious human sacrifice becomes, in a technical sense, both normal and moral."

I dare say — in fact I know — I am absurdly old-fashioned in my ideas; but I state almost without hesitation that I do not see eye to eye with Mr. Seabrook over his favourite tipple. With regard to human sacrifices I am a frank reactionary, standing nearer, I should imagine, to the position of the late Mrs. Humphry Ward than to that of Mr. W. B. Seabrook. Nor do I want any of my female relations to go and live in lonely cottages and distil venom or eat beetles and mice. Any girl who insists on going into the heart of Central America and being immolated by a noble, bronze-limbed Indian on a sacrificial stone appears to me to be lacking in refinement and gentility. She may think it gives her harmony and poise, and feel at the moment when the gleaming knife falls a tranquil sweetness and oneness with the whole of universal nature from the beginning of time until now. But I think she is a silly egg.

I suppose it is a kind of return to Nature, comparable to the feeling which inspired the poets of the Lake School.

But Wordsworth never lapped blood. I think the circle is too complete.

And if Macaulay's cultured New Zealander ever comes to look at what was London from Westminster, or Charing Cross, or St. Paul's Bridge, I think it would be a great pity if he found a lot of Anglo-Saxon aborigines practising mumbo-jumbo amongst the stones.

CHRISTOPHER DARLINGTON MORLEY

(born 1890)

Christopher Morley is an American, born at Harvard, U.S.A.
He made his name first as a novelist, but has also many essays
and several plays to his credit. He spent three years at Oxford,
but later returned to America. His style is pleasant and vivid.

ON DOORS

The opening and closing of doors are the most sig-
nificant actions of man's life. What a mystery lies in
doors!

No man knows what awaits him when he opens a
door. Even the most familiar room, where the clock
ticks and the hearth glows red at dusk, may harbour
surprises. The plumber may actually have called (while
you were out) and fixed that leaking faucet. The cook
may have had a fit of the vapours and demanded her
passports. The wise man opens his front door with
humility and a spirit of acceptance.

Which one of us has not sat in some anteroom and
watched the inscrutable panels of a door that was full
of meaning? Perhaps you were waiting to apply for a
job; perhaps you had some " deal " you were ambitious
to put over. You watched the confidential stenographer
flit in and out, carelessly turning that mystic portal
which, to you, revolved on hinges of fate. And then the
young woman said, " Mr. Cranberry will see you now."

As you grasped the knob the thought flashed, " When I open this door again, what will have happened?"

There are many kinds of doors. Revolving doors for hotels, shops, and public buildings. These are typical of the brisk, bustling ways of modern life. Can you imagine John Milton or William Penn skipping through a revolving door? Then there are the curious little slatted doors that still swing outside de-natured bar-rooms and extend only from shoulder to knee. There are trap-doors, sliding doors, double doors, stage doors, prison doors, glass doors. But the symbol and mystery of a door resides in its quality of concealment. A glass door is not a door at all, but a window. The meaning of a door is to hide what lies inside; to keep the heart in suspense.

Also, there are many ways of opening doors. There is the cheery push of elbow with which the waiter shoves open the kitchen door when he bears in your tray of supper. There is the suspicious and tentative with-drawal of a door before the unhappy book agent or peddler. There is the genteel and carefully modulated recession with which footmen swing wide the oaken barriers of the great. There is the sympathetic and awful silence of the dentist's maid who opens the door into the operating room, and, without speaking, implies that the doctor is ready for you. There is the brisk cataclysmic opening of a door when the nurse comes in, very early in the morning — " It's a boy!"

Doors are the symbol of privacy, of retreat, of the mind's escape into blissful quietude or sad secret struggle. A room without doors is not a room, but a hallway. No matter where he is, a man can make himself at home behind a closed door. The mind works best behind closed doors. Men are not horses to be herded together. Dogs know the meaning and anguish of doors. Have you ever noticed a puppy yearning at a shut portal? It is a symbol of human life.

The opening of doors is a mystic act: it has in it some flavour of the unknown, some sense of moving into a new moment, a new pattern of the human rigmarole. It includes the highest glimpses of mortal gladness: reunions, reconciliations, the bliss of lovers long parted. Even in sadness, the opening of a door may bring relief: it changes and redistributes human forces. But the closing of doors is far more terrible. It is a confession of finality. Every door closed brings something to an end. And there are degrees of sadness in the closing of doors. A door slammed is a confession of weakness. A door gently shut is often the most tragic gesture in life. Every one knows the seizure of anguish that comes just after the closing of a door, when the loved one is still near, without sound of voice, and yet already far away.

The opening and closing of doors is a part of the stern fluency of life. Life will not stay still and let us alone. We are continually opening doors with hope, closing them with despair. Life lasts not much longer than a pipe of tobacco, and destiny knocks us out like the ashes.

The closing of a door is irrevocable. It snaps the pack-thread of the heart. It is no avail to reopen, to go back. Pinero spoke nonsense when he made Paula Tanqueray say, " The future is only the past entered through another gate." Alas, there is no other gate. When the door is shut, it is shut forever. There is no other entrance to that vanished pulse of time. " The moving finger writes, and having writ ——"

There is a certain kind of door-shutting that will come

to us all. The kind of door-shutting that is done very quietly, with the sharp click of the latch to break the stillness. They will think then, one hopes, of our unfulfilled decencies rather than of our pluperfected misdemeanours. Then they will go out and close the door.

NOTES AND EXERCISES

NOTES AND EXERCISES

FRANCIS BACON: *Of Truth* and *Of Studies*.

These essays are printed as they were when they first appeared. Notice that the spelling is sometimes very different from ours of to-day: also that Bacon made much more use of capital letters than we do now, and that he punctuates quite differently from the modern style. You will also find, if you read the essays thoughtfully, that the words Bacon uses have not always the same meaning as they have nowadays.

Note how concisely these essays are written. A good deal of thought is necessary to follow the line of Bacon's thought; you will find that it is quite impossible to read the essays rapidly.

Exercises:

(1) Turn into modern English the first part of the essay " Of Truth ", down to " in varied lights ".

(2) Find modern equivalents for the following words, as used by Bacon: Valuations, indisposition, affections, adventures, swelling, charity; ornament, retiring, humour, crafty, curiously, conference, reins, demonstrations, receipt.

(3) Write an essay on " Truth ", basing your work upon Bacon's essays, but using it merely as a guide and a source of ideas.

(4) Similarly, write an essay on " The Value of Study ".

(5) Write a short essay " Of Sleep ", imitating the style of Bacon. Use modern spelling, but Bacon's method of punctuation, if you can discover what it was. (You will find this a difficult exercise.)

(6) Learn by heart the passage from the essay " Of Studies " beginning with " Some bookes are to be Tasted " and ending " Able to Contend ".

ABRAHAM COWLEY: *Of Myself.*

Notice how greatly Cowley's style differs from that of Bacon. His English is much less condensed; instead of simply giving a summary of his thoughts, he enlarges on his ideas sufficiently to allow the reader to follow very easily. Yet an essayist of a century later would probably have recounted more events and fewer feelings. Cowley almost always quotes some verse in his essays; but we must remember that he was a poet as well as an essayist. The spelling and punctuation of this essay have been modernized.

Exercises:

(1) Find the meaning of the following words as used in this essay: Disparagement, scandalous, bent, temper, dispensed, immature, numbers, affections, adulterate, compassed.

(2) From the material in this essay, write a brief account of Cowley's boyhood and youth.

(3) Examine the verse quotations, and show why Cowley introduced them into the essay.

(4) Write an essay " On Myself ", using this essay as a guide.

SIR RICHARD STEELE: *A Ramble from Richmond to London*, *The Spectator Club*, and *Sir Roger de Coverley's Portrait Gallery*.

These essays are printed with their original spelling, punctuation, and use of capital letters. Note that the system of punctuation employed is not the same as that of Bacon, but much more akin to our own. Notice also that the use of capital letters is much more systematic, and the vocabulary less strange.

Exercises:

(1) Examine the essays carefully, and try to explain Steele's system of punctuation and his use of capital letters.

(2) Find the meaning of the following words as used in these essays: Busy, humour, purveyors, dark-house, slattern, intelligence, discovered, cant, fraternity, chequered, bell-man; singular, perverse, cast, quorum, humoursome, disinterested, indefatigable, perspicuity, invincible, assurance, vindication, obsequious, preferment, probity; predecessor, lists, laudable, portion, romp, retrieved, integrity, signification.

(3) Make a list of words not spelt in the modern way.

(4) Write an essay on " Markets ", using the information in the essay on Steele's ramble from Richmond to London.

(5) Write a description of a day's journey by road or river.

(6) Find out what you can about the places mentioned in the Richmond essay.

(7) Find out what you can about the proper names mentioned in the essay on the Spectator Club.

(8) Invent an imaginary club of this kind, including a soldier, a sailor, an airman, a motorist, a wireless

announcer, a teacher, a detective, and any others you wish, and describe the members briefly, inventing suitable names for them.

(9) Rewrite the essay on the Portrait Gallery as it might be to-day.

JOSEPH ADDISON: *Sir Roger and Will Wimble, The Autobiography of a Shilling*, and *A Vision of Mirzah*.

These essays, like those of Steele, are printed as they originally appeared. Note how closely Addison's style resembles that of Steele; it has sometimes less vigour and more daintiness, but otherwise they are very much alike indeed.

Exercises:

(1) Find the meaning of the following words as used in these essays: Jack, shuttlecock, sumptuous, uncapable (what is the modern form of this word?), physick; complaisance, paradox, delirium, apothecary, Ordinary, inveigle, gallant, disinherited, gamester, melancholy; contemplation, paradise, genius, soliloquies, scymetars (what is the modern spelling?), prospect, harpies, dissipated, mansions.

(2) Write a letter from Will Wimble to a friend, describing his visit to Sir Roger.

(3) Write an essay on " Sir Roger Listens In ".

(4) What historical events are referred to in the " Autobiography of a Shilling "? Give a very brief account of the period covered by this essay.

(5) Try to explain the " fatal catastrophe " mentioned in the last paragraph of that essay.

(6) Write an essay on " The Autobiography of a One Pound Note ". (Remember that its experiences would probably be very different from those of a shilling.)

(7) Give a full and clear explanation of the allegory in the " Vision of Mirzah ".

(8) Read Rossetti's " Blessed Damozel ", and compare its imagery with that of this essay.

(9) In the same style, write an account of an imaginary vision dealing with the struggle between the forces of good and evil.

ALEXANDER POPE: *On Epic Poetry.*

Pope, in this essay, is satirizing the many epic-writers, good and bad (mostly the latter), of his day. In justice to him we must remember that he himself was a poet of very great ability; and he was always impatient of anything that fell short of perfection. This essay, of course, must not be taken literally; it is an excellent example of sarcasm.

Exercises:

(1) Make a list of famous epic poems, and find out what was the subject of each of them.

(2) Find out what you can about all the proper names in this essay.

(3) Summarize what Pope really thought about writing an epic poem.

(4) In imitation of the style of this essay, write " A Recipe to make a Popular Song ".

(5) Read a description of a football or cricket match in a newspaper, and then in a similar style write a criticism of a poem or essay which you know well.

OLIVER GOLDSMITH: *The Man in Black, Beau Tibbs,* and *Beau Tibbs at Home.*

Notice what an easy natural style Goldsmith has, and how much more kindly his outlook on his fellow-men is than that of Johnson. Notice also his habit of recording details, and how he picks out exactly the right details to record. Examine closely his description of Beau Tibbs, and see how methodically he goes about it.

Exercises:

(1) Compare the style of Goldsmith with that of Johnson, pointing out their resemblances and their differences.

(2) Summarize the essay on the Man in Black, using only the simplest language.

(3) Write an account of an imaginary interview between the Man in Black and Beau Tibbs.

(4) Try to describe Beau Tibbs as Addison or Steele might have done it.

(5) Tell the story of the match incident as the old sailor saw it.

(6) Write an essay on " Impostors ".

CHARLES LAMB: *Mrs. Battle's Opinions on Whist, A Dissertation upon Roast Pig, Old China,* and *Dream-Children.*

The style of these essays comes very near perfection. Note how effectively Lamb makes use of humour and pathos, and how simply he gains his effects; there is never the slightest sense of strain in Lamb's writing.

Exercises:

(1) Write a sketch of Lamb's character, as shown by these essays.

(2) Describe Mrs. Battle as she might be to-day. (Remember that to-day she would probably have different tastes, and would certainly play different games.)

(3) Discuss Lamb's use of detail.

(4) Write an essay on " Indoor Games ".

(5) In the manner of the essay on Roast Pig, write a tale to explain the origin of writing. (Then read Kipling's tales, *How the Alphabet was Made* and *The First Letter*, in the *Just-So Stories*.)

(6) Write an essay on " The Pleasures of the Table ".

(7) In the form of a dialogue, write an account of an interview between Bridget and Mrs. Battle.

(8) Tell the story of the Willow-pattern Plate as you think Lamb might have told it.

(9) Write an essay on " The Joys of Poverty ".

(10) Write an essay on " Old Toys ".

WILLIAM HAZLITT: *John Cavanagh* and *On Familiar Style.*

These two essays are on very different subjects; but note how clear and vivid they both are, and how plain Hazlitt always makes his meaning. (Note, however, that it is not quite certain that the essay on John Cavanagh is really the work of Hazlitt, though it probably is.)

Exercises:

(1) Examine the first essay carefully, and try to find out how Hazlitt makes the picture of Cavanagh so clear.

(2) Write an essay in praise of a great footballer, cricketer, or hockey-player you have seen.

(3) Summarize the essay on " Familiar Style ".

(4) What are Hazlitt's views on (*a*) long words, (*b*) slang, (*c*) accuracy, (*d*) exaggeration?

(5) In the light of this essay, write criticisms of the styles of Steele, Leigh Hunt, and Thackeray.

JAMES LEIGH HUNT: *On the Graces and Anxieties of Pig-Driving* and *On Getting Up on Cold Mornings*.

There is little to note about these essays, save that they are good examples of the light essay, and much more like the essays at the end of this book than like those at the beginning.

Exercises:

(1) Pick out as many figures of speech as you can in the first essay, and consider their appropriateness.

(2) Write a light essay on " Taking the Dog for a Walk ".

(3) In the second essay, look up all the words you do not understand in a dictionary, and criticize Leigh Hunt's use of them.

(4) Write an essay " In Praise of Laziness ".

THOMAS DE QUINCEY: *On the Knocking at the Gate in Macbeth*.

If you have not read *Macbeth* before reading this essay, you must read at least the first three scenes of Act II. De Quincey's vivid imagination made him well able to picture and understand the feelings of others, even in very unusual circumstances; and this essay is therefore a valuable piece of dramatic criticism.

Exercises:

(1) Summarize De Quincey's thoughts on the knocking at the gate.

(2) Write a criticism of the most exciting scene in any play of Shakespeare that you have read.

(3) Do you think it is more effective to see or to read a play? Give the reasons for your answer.

THOMAS CARLYLE: *Sir Jabesh Windbag*.

Notice Carlyle's odd but vigorous style, and his rather unusual punctuation and use of capital letters. His style should be imitated only for special purposes; it is not to be taken as a general model.

Exercises:

(1) Try to pick out the peculiarities of Carlyle's style, and to see how he gains his vigorous effects.

(2) Find out what you can about the proper names in this essay.

(3) Sir Jabesh Windbag was not a real person, but a composite picture of various politicians of whom Carlyle did not approve. Write a similar description of some class of whom you yourself do not approve.

(4) Give Carlyle's views on Oliver Cromwell, showing in what respects he approved of him and in what respects he disapproved of him.

(5) What proofs does this essay give of Carlyle's very wide education?

THOMAS BABINGTON MACAULAY: *Oliver Goldsmith*.

Note the clear thought, clear expression, and wealth of telling detail in this essay. (The information given in this essay may be taken as accurate.)

Exercises:

(1) From the information in this essay, write a brief life of Oliver Goldsmith.

(2) Re-read the three essays by Goldsmith in this book, and estimate how far he was writing of himself in these essays.

(3) Write an essay on " A Man is Known by his Works ".

(4) Dryden said:

> " Great wits are sure to madness close allied,
> And thin partitions do their bounds divide."

Discuss this statement.

ROBERT LOUIS STEVENSON: *Walking Tours, A Plea for Gas Lamps*, and *Child's Play*.

Remember that these essays were written primarily for the benefit of young people, and note how simple the style is. Note also how clear the reasoning is, and how easily it may be followed.

Exercises:

(1) How does Stevenson's idea of a walking tour compare with that of the " hikers " of to-day?

(2) How far were Stevenson's views affected by the age in which he lived?

(3) Compare Stevenson's essay on " Child's Play " with Lamb's essay on " Dream-Children ".

(4) Read Wordsworth's " Ode on the Intimations of Immortality in early Childhood ", and compare the views expressed in it with those in this essay.

(5) Write an essay on " The Progress of Civilization ".

AUGUSTINE BIRRELL: *Old Booksellers*.

Notice how Birrell's own obvious interest in his subject gives life to what might have been merely a rather dull catalogue of unknown names.

Exercises:

(1) Compare the ideas expressed in this essay with those in Bacon's essay " Of Studies ".

(2) Write an essay on " Shopkeepers ".

(3) In the style of the quotations from Dunton, write comments on people you yourself know or have known — for example, your teachers (but perhaps you had better not let them see all the comments!).

(4) If you can find a very old newspaper, write an essay based on the advertisements in it.

EDWARD VERRALL LUCAS: *Her Royal 'Tumnal Tintiness.*

This is one of the most charming essays on a dog ever written. Notice how the author's love of dogs shows through his humorous remarks.

Exercises:

(1) Compare the style of this essay with that of one by (*a*) Lamb, (*b*) Goldsmith, (*c*) Leigh Hunt. Which does it resemble most closely?

(2) Write an essay on some animal of which you are very fond, in the style of this essay.

(3) Try to turn into verse the translation of the Chinese poem quoted in this essay.

HILAIRE BELLOC: *On Cheeses.*

Note how Mr. Belloc adds to the humorous effect by his digressions and his use of odd words.

Exercises:

(1) What details in this essay show that it was meant for publication in a newspaper?

(2) Do you agree with the author's remarks on punctuation? Give reasons for your answer.

(3) Make a list of as many kinds of sweets as you can; then write an essay " On Sweets " modelled on this essay.

GILBERT KEITH CHESTERTON: *On Running after One's Hat.*

As the title suggests, this essay is not meant to be taken seriously. It perhaps adds to the fun to know that Chesterton was very stout and not very tall; one could not imagine him *enjoying* a run after his hat!

Exercises:

(1) Read this essay carefully, and try to find out just why it is so amusing.

(2) Think of the most amusing thing that you have ever seen, describe it, and show why it made you laugh.

(3) Write a humorous essay " On Missing the Train ".

(4) Write an essay on " The Cruelty of Laughter ".

ROBERT LYND: *The Unexpected.*

This essay is of a type that has become much more popular in recent years than formerly — the nature essay. The author knows a very great deal about birds; yet his essay is made so interesting that even one who knows very little about birds can enjoy it.

Exercises:

(1) Do you consider that this essay has the best possible title? If not, try to suggest a better one.

(2) Write an essay on " Joys of the Countryside ".

(3) Compare the views expressed in this essay with the saying that " Half the pleasure in a thing is the joy of looking forward to it ".

EDMUND VALPY KNOX: *Witches and Whatnot.*

Conversation is one of the most difficult things to write; but notice how vivid and natural the conversation is in this essay. The essay is really a criticism of Mr. Seabrook's book, and the fact that it has been made amusing sharpens rather than blunts the edge of the criticism.

Exercises:

(1) Write down, as accurately as you can, a conversation which you have actually heard. Be careful not to use the word " said " too often; if you study this essay carefully, you will find out how to avoid it.

(2) Write an essay on " Magic, Ancient and Modern ".

(3) What is meant by the " change between our present attitude and that of Victorian literature "?

CHRISTOPHER MORLEY: *On Doors.*

Notice how closely the author keeps to the subject of his essay. This will strike you very clearly if you compare it with Mr. Belloc's essay " On Cheeses ", which is an example of the " discursive essay ".

Exercises:

(1) What words or phrases in this essay might lead you to suspect, if you did not know, that it was written by an American?

(2) Expand and explain the last paragraph.

(3) Write an essay " On Windows ".